Maestà Pa

Alien Investigation

Translated from French by
Talia Ustundag.

1

Contents.

Foreword.

If the Roswell accident is considered a
great turning point in the history of ufology, the
year 2020 would be its passage from a secondary
road to a fast lane. Indeed, in 2020 everything
seems to have accelerated, between the projects
of the shadow government's agenda, the
UFO sightings rise and break records. For
example, in April 2020, the Pentagon declared
that the UFO phenomenon was real. The
United States Department of Defense thus
formalizes belatedly, what many
have observed for centuries.

"The idea that the order and the precision of the universe in all its innumerable aspects would be the result of a blind coincidence is as incredible as if after the explosion of a printing press all the characters would fall on the ground in the order of a dictionary."

Albert Einstein

Introduction.

This book, divided into three parts, will attempt in the first part, entitled "Evidence", answers the question, "Are we alone in Universe?". "Evidence" is a collection of verified evidences, anecdotes, testimonials and observations on the UFO and extraterrestrial phenomenon.

The second part entitled "Dialectic" tries to answer the same question but from a more philosophical way. This part regroups different theories, hypotheses and reflections on the subject.

The third part that I named "Contact" will try to answer the questions "why is there still no official contact with the extraterrestrials? And what would happen to our society, after a contact with one or more extraterrestrial civilizations?

"Many facts are rejected because they disturb established reasoning"

The Morning of the magicians.
L.Pauwels/Jacques Bergiers.

Chapter I. Evidence.

"Some books are like master paintings, they are only appreciated, at their true value, once their authors die out".

Maestà Pastore.

I.1. Statistical proof.

Let's start by situating ourselves, by addressing the topic with some general information.
Our planet is lucky to be located in a peaceful suburb of our galaxy " the Milky Way ".
The Milky Way which contains between 150 to 250 billion stars. Each of these stars possesses, according to the most pessimists, between one to three planets orbiting around them. Specialists believe that they would have at least 1.6 times more planets than of stars in the Milky Way. In other words, 150 billion multiplied by 1.6, that makes us 240 billion planets. Currently, dozen exoplanets have been identified as being, in the habitable zone of their solar system, so not too far or too close of their sun, and therefore conducive to development of intelligent life. The

latest estimates suggest, that there would be at least 500 million planets located in the habitable zones of our galaxy. Which is Just **"Huge!"**.

The Andromeda Galaxy has 1 trillion stars. The Triangulum galaxy 40 billion stars. The Large Magellanic Cloud has 30 billion stars, the Galaxy M51 has 100 billion stars, the Galaxy M64 has 100 billion stars, the Galaxy M104 also called the Sombrero Galaxy has 100 billion stars. The astronomers estimate the number of galaxies, in the known universe, at between 100 and 200 billion.

The first proof of the existence of extraterrestrials is therefore of a statistical nature.

Billions of planets and galaxies, and **we are alone in this vast universe?**
The notion just seems absurd.

I.2. Cave paintings.

Cave paintings are made of natural pigments. They stayed unaltered and have survived the wear and tear of time and erosion. They are dated from - 5000, -10000, or older.
Our ancestors used to represent their experiences with drawings and carvings inside their homes.
In these prehistoric caves dating from the Neolithic, Mesolithic or Late Paleolithic period, between representations of everyday scenes, hunting scenes or representations of animals, strange humanoids silhouettes, men in spacesuits and flying objects defy all logic.
Specialists say that, to paint this kind of object, according to the official historical timeline yet unknown, our ancestors must have or had

experienced these facts or had an overflowing imagination.

From Australian Aborigines to Teotihuacan, through India, Europe and Africa, representations are far too numerous on Earth than to be attributed to the simple chance.

India, Chhattisgarh.

Long before the Sumerians invented writing, the inhabitants of this central region from India had already painted. We can see in their caves, men or humanoids in spacesuit and flying objects in the shape of disk. More than 10,000 years old, the paintings seem to represent extraterrestrials. The inhabitants of neighboring villages make the link between cave paintings and the history of their ancestors, the people of "Rohela", which means "those of small size". These beings would have visited the Chhattisgarh ancestors using a disc-shaped flying ship. The natives wanted to proof with their way of praying, which would be inherited from these people who came from the stars **"the Rohelas"**. According to the aborigines, The **Rohelas** would have left with two villager who never returned.

Australia.

Surprisingly, Australian Aborigines have decorated their caves with representations of similar beings, who also came from the sky. The most famous are those of Kimberley. According to Aboriginal myths these beings called "Wandijna", would be at the origin of the creation of the world, "at the time of dreams", period during which the gods would have been on Earth.
Their cosmogony tells us about a strange battle between the god of Earth and the god of heaven. In this story, the god of the Earth is defeated by the onslaught of devastating heat emanating from the ship of the god of heaven and "The wandijnas" they are also called "spirits of Ancestors" withdrew from the face of the Earth, at the same time as "the time of dreams" ended.

In another version the God of dreamtime "Altjira" created Earth and retreated in the heavens. This cosmogony, like that of the rohelas, presents many similarities with "the ancient astronaut theory".

15

France

Similar representations are observable
in certain caves in the south of France. The caves
of Pech-Merle, Cougnac,
Lombrives, three brothers and Cambarelles
are the most known.
The rock paintings of the caves of Pech-
Merle and de Cougnac, distant from each other
by only 40 km, seem to represent the same facts.
Between the paintings depicting animals, a
character with slanted eyes,
large round head without ears and
pierced by multiple spears looks out of place.
above this curious character, we can
observe a UFO. Is this the representation of a
battle between our ancestors and the
extraterrestrials of the UFO?

In the cave of Lombrives in Niaux, we can
observe symbols representing flying objects.
Some of them are accompanied by dotted signs,
suggesting the idea of a movement.

In the cave of the three brothers in Saint-Girons,
we can observe the engraving of a sorcerer half
human half animal and characters
in modern clothes. Can we talk about
time travelers?

In the Cambarelles cave in the Dordogne.
We can observe the representation of
multiple saucer-shaped UFOs.

Northern Italy, near Brescia.

In the cave of Val-Camonica, on the paintings
caves dating from -10000, we can
observe the representation of two people in
spacesuits. Former Astronauts or time travelers?

**Spain, between Madrid and Zaragoza at
Guadalajara.**

In the caves of Los Casares, on the paintings
dating from -15000, we can
observe aliens seen at multiple
times on Earth "the greys".

Algeria.

The Tassili n'Ajjer plateau is an immense
plateau of 72000km² grouping multiple
prehistoric rock carvings and paintings.
The one that interests us, dates from - 10000 and
is known as the Tassili fresco. We
can observe a massive figure at the head
round wearing a diving suit. The character

looks a lot like our modern astronauts.

Peru at Toro Muerto.

On cave paintings dating from -14000,
we can observe characters with
halos covering their heads and UFOs.

Mexico to Queretaro.

On hieroglyphics, we can observe the
representation of four figurines below
an oval object like a flying saucer.

Uzbekistan.

In the Fergana Valley. On their cave paintings
dating from - 10000, we can observe characters
in spacesuits. Right here also we can ask
ourselves the same questions, former astronauts
or temporal travelers?

This list is of course not exhaustive,
many sites around the world display
proudly the same prehistoric testimonies.

What to remember?

they are too many to be ignored, and too similar only to be considered as chance. Our ancestors separated by thousands of miles, by seas and oceans could not have imagined these characters, but well experienced the same facts that they would have simply represented afterwards.

"The doubt of the spirit leads to manifest the truth".

Aristotle.

I.3. In the holy books.

For a discerning eye, holy writings abound stories and cosmic anecdotes. Here are some examples:

The book of Enoch, book of the watchers, chapter 13, verse 9 to 25:

Let us first recall who Enoch was. Enoch was the great grandfather of the prophet Noah. His son was Methuselah, Mathusalem for the Hebrews, his grandson was Lamesh and Lamesh's son was Noah.
Enoch was himself a prophet, the seventh after Adam, he is for Muslims the prophet "Idriss", and is mentioned in verse 56 of the surah "Mary" of the Holy Quran, God asks

to the Prophet Muhammad, "And mentions Idriss,in the book. It was someone who spoke the right words ".

The book of Enoch is an apocryphal book, it is therefore not part of the canon of the Church. the
prophet Enoch lived during the period antediluvian, 72 fallen angels and giants called "Nefirin" It's in this context that he explains his visions and travels.

Here is one of them:

"9 the vision caused me to fly and lifted me upward, and bore me into heaven. And I went in till I drew nigh to a wall which is built of crystals and surrounded by tongues of fire: and it began to affright
10 me. And I went into the tongues of fire and drew nigh to a large house which was built of crystals: and the walls of the house were like a tesselated floor (made) of crystals, and its groundwork was
11 of crystal. Its ceiling was like the path of the stars and the lightnings, and between them were

12 fiery cherubim, and their heaven was (clear as) water. A flaming fire surrounded the walls, and its
13 portals blazed with fire. And I entered into that house, and it was hot as fire and cold as ice: there
14 were no delights of life therein: fear covered me, and trembling got hold upon me. And as I quaked
15 and trembled, I fell upon my face. And I beheld a vision, And lo! there was a second house, greater
16 than the former, and the entire portal stood open before me, and it was built of flames of fire. And in every respect it so excelled in splendor and magnificence and extent that I cannot describe to
17 you its splendor and its extent. And its floor was of fire, and above it were lightnings and the path
18 of the stars, and its ceiling also was flaming fire. And I looked and saw therein a lofty throne: its appearance was as crystal, and the wheels thereof as the shining sun, and there was the vision of
19 cherubim. And from underneath the throne came streams of flaming fire so that I could not look

20 thereon. And the Great Glory sat thereon, and His raiment shone more brightly than the sun and

21 was whiter than any snow. None of the angels could enter and could behold His face by reason

22 of the magnificence and glory and no flesh could behold Him. The flaming fire was round about Him, and a great fire stood before Him, and none around could draw nigh Him: ten thousand times

23 ten thousand (stood) before Him, yet He needed no counselor. And the most holy ones who were

24 nigh to Him did not leave by night nor depart from Him. And until then I had been prostrate on my face, trembling: and the Lord called me with His own mouth, and said to me: ' Come hither,

25 Enoch, and hear my word.' And one of the holy ones came to me and waked me, and He made me rise up and approach the door: and I bowed my face downwards.

Ezekiel's vision, Old Testament, Book of prophets:

1 In my thirtieth year, in the fourth month on the fifth day, while I was among the exiles by the Kebar River, the heavens were opened and I saw visions of God.

2 On the fifth of the month—it was the fifth year of the exile of King Jehoiachin— 3 the word of the Lord came to Ezekiel the priest, the son of Buzi, by the Kebar River in the land of the Babylonians.[a] There the hand of the Lord was on him.

4 I looked, and I saw a windstorm coming out of the north—an immense cloud with flashing lightning and surrounded by brilliant light. The center of the fire looked like glowing metal, 5 and in the fire was what looked like four living creatures. In appearance their form was human, 6 but each of them had four faces and four wings. 7 Their legs were straight; their feet were like those of a calf and gleamed like burnished bronze. 8 Under their wings on their four sides they had human hands. All four of them had faces and wings, 9 and the wings of one touched the wings of another. Each one went straight ahead; they did not turn as they moved.

10 Their faces looked like this: Each of the four had the face of a human being, and on the right side each had the face of a lion, and on the left the face of an ox; each also had the face of an eagle. 11 Such were their faces. They each had two wings spreading out upward, each wing touching that of the creature on either side; and each had two other wings covering its body. 12 Each one went straight ahead. Wherever the spirit would go, they would go, without turning as they went. 13 The appearance of the living creatures was like burning coals of fire or like torches. Fire moved back and forth among the creatures; it was bright, and lightning flashed out of it. 14 The creatures sped back and forth like flashes of lightning.

15 As I looked at the living creatures, I saw a wheel on the ground beside each creature with its four faces. 16 This was the appearance and structure of the wheels: They sparkled like topaz, and all four looked alike. Each appeared to be made like a wheel intersecting a wheel. 17 As they moved, they would go in any one of the four directions the creatures faced; the wheels did not change direction as the creatures went. 18 Their rims were high and awesome, and all four rims were full of eyes all around.

19 When the living creatures moved, the wheels beside them moved; and when the living creatures rose from the ground, the wheels also rose. 20 Wherever the spirit would go, they would go, and the wheels would rise along with them, because the spirit of the living creatures was in the wheels. 21 When the creatures moved, they also moved; when the creatures stood still, they also stood still; and when the creatures rose from the ground, the wheels rose along with them, because the spirit of the living creatures was in the wheels.

22 Spread out above the heads of the living creatures was what looked something like a vault, sparkling like crystal, and awesome. 23 Under the vault their wings were stretched out one toward the other, and each had two wings covering its body. 24 When the creatures moved, I heard the sound of their wings, like the roar of rushing waters, like the voice of the Almighty, like the tumult of an army. When they stood still, they lowered their wings.

25 Then there came a voice from above the vault over their heads as they stood with lowered wings. 26 Above the vault over their heads was what looked like a throne of lapis lazuli, and high

above on the throne was a figure like that of a man. 27 I saw that from what appeared to be his waist up he looked like glowing metal, as if full of fire, and that from there down he looked like fire; and brilliant light surrounded him. 28 Like the appearance of a rainbow in the clouds on a rainy day, so was the radiance around him.

This was the appearance of the likeness of the glory of the Lord. When I saw it, I fell facedown, and I heard the voice of one speaking.

The Psalms of David 18.6 to 18.20:

6 In my distress I called to the Lord;
   I cried to my God for help.
From his temple he heard my voice;
   my cry came before him, into his ears.
7 The earth trembled and quaked,
   and the foundations of the mountains shook;
   they trembled because he was angry.
8 Smoke rose from his nostrils;
   consuming fire came from his mouth,
   burning coals blazed out of it.
9 He parted the heavens and came down;
   dark clouds were under his feet.
10 He mounted the cherubim and flew;
   he soared on the wings of the wind.

11 He made darkness his covering, his canopy
around him— the dark rain clouds of the sky.
12 Out of the brightness of his presence clouds
advanced, with hailstones and bolts of lightning.
13 The Lord thundered from heaven;
    the voice of the Most High resounded.
14 He shot his arrows and scattered the enemy,
    with great bolts of lightning he routed them.
15 The valleys of the sea were exposed
    and the foundations of the earth laid bare at
your rebuke, Lord, at the blast of breath from
your nostrils.
16 He reached down from on high and took
hold of me; he drew me out of deep waters.
17 He rescued me from my powerful enemy,
    from my foes, who were too strong for me.
18 They confronted me in the day of my disaster,
    but the Lord was my support.
19 He brought me out into a spacious place;
    he rescued me because he delighted in me.
20 The Lord has dealt with me according to my
righteousness; according to the cleanness of my
hands he has rewarded me.

Holy Quran Surah Al-Isra, Verse 70:

Indeed, we have dignified the children of Adam,
carried them on land and sea, granted them good
and lawful provisions, and privileged them far
above many of Our creatures.

Tibetan Dzyan, Stance 1.2.:

The Earth says: "Lord with a luminous face, my
house is empty... Send your Sons to populate
this Wheel. You sent your Seven Sons to
Lord of Wisdom. Seven times he sees you closer
of him, seven times more he feels you. You
defended your Servants, the little Rings, to seize
of your Light and your Heat, to intercept your
great Kindness in its passage. send them
now to your Servant."

In the Hindu holy book, The Mahabharata:

"At one time, when King Citaketu was traveling
in outer space with a shiny airplane given to him
by Lord Vishnu, he saw Lord Siva... The arrows
made by Lord Siva resembled fiery rays
emanating from the solar globe and
covered the three residential aircraft which
could then no longer be seen. »

Srimad Bhagasvatam

"Here is now the Great Chariot of Vata!" The
destruction comes with him and thunder is his
noise. The heavens he touches, making the sky
glow light (a proud red glow) and swirls
dust on the Earth.

Rig-Veda.

"An air chariot, the Pushpaka transports
many people to the capital of Ayodhya.
The sky is full of flying machines
suspended, as black as the night, but full
of lights with a yellow aera."

Mahavira.

"The cruel Salva arrived mounted on the chariot
Saubha who could go anywhere, and from him
he killed many valiant young Vrishni and
badly devastated all the gardens of the city."

The Mahabharata

There is a testimony of the hero Krishna who
suggests modern weapons. As he climbed
in the sky to pursue Salva:

31

He clung to his Saubha in the sky at a
one step ahead... He threw rockets at me,
missiles, spears, spikes, axes,
javelins, torches, and without any pause...the
sky...seemed to contain hundreds of suns,
a hundred moons... and myriads of stars.
At that time, it was no longer possible to do the
difference between day and night.

The Mahabharata

"The plane occupied by Salva was very
mysterious. He was so extraordinary that
sometimes the plane was visible and sometimes
not, and the warriors of the Yadu dynasty were
disrupted by this special aircraft. Sometimes they
could see the plane on the ground, sometimes
fly in the sky, sometimes stay on the
mountain top and sometimes floating
on the water. The wonderful plane was flying in
the sky like a swirling brand."

Bhaktivedanta.

"The Puspaka vehicle that looked like the sun
and the belonging to my brother had been
brought by powerful Raya, this excellent and
powerful vehicle could go anywhere...he looked
like a bright cloud in the sky."

"And King Rama had it, and the excellent vehicle with commands of Ragira, It went higher in the atmosphere."

Ramayana.

"Solid and durable must be the body of the Vimana, like a great flying bird made of matter light. Inside must be put the motor mercury with his metallic heating device below.
Thanks to the latent power in the mercury which allows movement, a man seated at interior can travel long distances in the sky. The movements of the Vimana are such that it can rise vertically, descend vertically, tilt forward and backward.
With the help of machines, human beings can fly through the air and eventually come back to the ground."

Sanskrit Samarangana Sutradhara.

"The privilege of using a flying machine is big. The knowledge of flight is found among the oldest of our heritages. A gift from "those who are higher". We got it of them in order to be able to save many lives".

I.4. The Dogon.

The Dogon are an ethnic group indigenous to the central plateau region of Mali, in West Africa. They amaze us with their cosmogony but more again with their astronomical knowledge.

According to their cosmogony, the God Amma would be the creator of the world. He would have drawn the Earth from a clay sausage. From this matter would be born, the eight "nommos", beings with magical powers, that gave birth to the eight Dogon tribes. Until nothing very special there. But here's where things get tough, the Dogon affirm that these "nomos" would have come from Sirius, and that Sirius is accompanied by another star. They do reference to the star Sirius B, this one is impossible to see

with the naked eye, Sirius B was discovered in
1836. The Dogon informed researchers of
others astronomical knowledge such as the four
main satellites of Jupiter, the rings of
Saturn, that the Earth revolves around the sun
and that it was part of the Milky Way, also that
the Milky Way was a Galaxy in spiral motion.
Apart from their great intriguing astronomical
knowledge, the Dogon, like the Australians
aborigines and the Indian Rohelas, assert that
their knowledge is due to extraterrestrial contact.
Some Western researchers claim that
the knowledge of the African tribe derives from
a cultural contamination. It is therefore during
the colonization that the Dogon would have
acquired these knowledges. This approach is very
egocentric and doesn't explain much. A
another hypothesis claims that the Dogon would
have been in contact with Muslim scholars or
even before the Muslim conquest with
ancient Egypt. Their knowledge would therefore
derive from these interactions. Although this
assumption is more plausible, it lacks concrete
evidence.

My position is that the Dogon, like others
primitive peoples, before and after them, were
visited by non-terrestrial entities.

I.5. Alien in art.

We can clearly observe on the
paintings and frescoes from the Middle Ages and
Renaissance, flying objects in the shape of
our modern UFOs.

Example 1:

Let's start with the most popular **"the Crucifix"**
by Visoki Decani. On The fresco dating from
1350, found in a monastery in Kosovo, two
strange flying objects attract attention and
seem to be out of context. On the corners
upper right and left, two people pilot, which
looks a lot like a flying capsule. A trail emanating
from objects is also visible. Flying objects are
therefore in movement. According to religious

art scholars, these objects would be the representation of the Moon and the Sun. We have a right to ask ourselves the following questions: Are the Moon and Sun inhabited? Or do the Sun and Moon need to be piloted by someone?

Why not simply consider these objects as two inhabited flying objects?

Example 2:

"The Annunciation, with Saint-Emidius" of 1486, painted by Carlo Crivelli and housed in the National Gallery in London.

We can observe a beam of light there emanating from a circular object surrounded by pointing to the Virgin Mary who is meditating. According to Renaissance art scholars, this scene represents the virgin Mary imbuing with the holy spirit and circular form between the clouds would be a white dove, symbolizing the incarnation. Here too we are entitled to ask us the question.

Why the painter would represent a dove in the shape of a rounded cloud?

Example 3:

A painting found in Belgium, near the castle
Conti d'Oultremont. We can see the
prophet Moses on a hill holding between his
hands the tablets of the ten commandments. the
prophet observes four oval objects in the
distance flying.

Example 4:

In Italy, in Florence, on the walls of the basilica
Santa Maria Maggiore. Masolino da Panicale's
painting, dated 1383, presents three flying discs.

On many other paintings dating from the Middle
age and Renaissance appear flying objects,
suspiciously resembling our modern UFOs. The
art specialists will systematically make the
connection with Christian symbolism, likening
UFOs to angels, demons, the Holy Spirit or
other Christian symbols while ufologists there
will see alien spaceships. Veracity
of one does not necessarily exclude the other,
why the artists of yesteryear would not share
their observations with us through the religious
symbolism. What shocks us in these works, is the
shape that these artists give to these flying
objects.

These representations are not only a few drops compared to the ocean of evidence that can be provided on this subject. They have their importance but should not be overestimated or minimized.

I.6. Mysterious relic.

Our Earth is full of mysterious objects,
discovered during archaeological excavations,
boreholes or in a completely harmless way.
These objects defy all logic, and some
of them more than others are troublesome,
because they discredit the current historical
chronology.
Napoleon Bonaparte said "History is the version
of past events that people have decided to agree
upon". These objects want to prove him right.
Let's start by listing some of them.
The Klerksdorp spheres, the Coso artifact, the
Antikythera mechanism, the London's hammer
in Texas, Baghdad battery, the Piri reis map, the
Aiud's artifact are the most popular, but

not the most surprising. There are others that are less known, which sometimes strangely disappear from museums. These out-of-place artifacts are constantly discredited by the scientific community because they disturb and discredit the currently accepted historical chronology. Here are some examples:

Massachusetts Dorchester, in 1851 during a mining operation, a 11.3 cm high vase is discovered. The vase is made of an alloy of zinc, It has a very high silver content and is decorated. The vase dated to 100,000 years ago while the first zinc alloys dated from 1804.

Massachusetts Springfield, 1851, Named De Witt, accidentally broke a piece of Quartz stone and discovered inside it, a 5 cm wrought iron nail. The stone is dated to a million years ago.

Nevada Treasure city, 1865, a piece of feldspar removed from a mine contained a oxidized threaded screw. The stone is dated to 21 million years ago.

Illinois Lawn Ridge, 1870, during a drilling operation, J.W.Moffit discovers a piece of an alloy of copper still unidentified in the 19th century. On one of its faces a crowned female face and on its second side there were two animals represented. The Coin is dated to age 150 000 years ago.

Illinois Morrisonville, 1891, S.W. Culp discovers by breaking a large block of coal a 25 cm long gold chain. Coal is the result of a "coalification" process that takes about 500 million years.

Oklahoma, 1912, a worker broke a large piece of coal, this one contained a metal tin can.

California Olancha, 1961, three co-owners from a mineral store bring back to Coso range a geode, in which two mysterious objects, looking like spark plugs of our modern cars. After analysis the objects are 500,000 years old. Exposed for three months at the California Museum, the object will eventually be sold. The buyer is anonymous.

South Africa, Western Transvaal, Ottosdale. Miners go up hundreds spherical metal objects from 2.5 to 10cm in diameter. These spheroids are steel blue color with red and sup reflections speckled with small white filament. They are made of nickel steel, so they are not natural. The objects seemed to be hollow but when opened, they contained a spongy material that evaporates on contact with oxygen. What is most surprising is the fact that these spheroids were extracted from a layer of rocks, geologically dated to 2.5 to 4.5 billion years ago. Curiously this corresponds to the age of our Earth

Another disturbing fact, the objects are exposed at the South African Museum in Klerksdorp and according to the curator of the R.Marx museum, the objects locked behind a window would turn slowly on their axes.

Turkey, Toprakkale, near the city of Van, end of the 1980s. In the ruins of the ancient city of Tuspa, A small statue 23 cm long and 9.3 cm high carved in volcanic rock is discovered. The statuette represents a pilot (head is broken) sitting in the cockpit of a craft having five propulsion engines and strongly resembling a modern rocket.

The discovery of this relic is in a first time disputed and is considered being a fake. Reviewed by the CEO museums of Turkey Alpay Pasinli, which deduces that the object is only a vulgar toy made of marble dust and plaster. The object will be removed from the museum. In the 90s the famous author Zecharia Sitchin visits the archaeological museums of Istanbul and not seeing this object, he asks the curator after this one. He explains to the author that after analysis the object was found out of context and therefore no longer exposed. Sitchin insists on seeing it, the object is brought to him on a velvet tray.

Zecharia Sitchin analyzes the object and for him the object is cut in volcanic rock and dates back 3000 years. The object was analyzed by many Western archaeologists, they are unanimous the object is not a fake and dates to 3000 years ago. Surprisingly the ship from Toprakkale resembles the Mayan "bas-relief" discovered in 1948 by doctor Alberto Ruz Lhuillier in Palenque, in a temple. The "bas-relief" dates from 683.

Ancient Egypt:

Built from 2.3 million blocks of stone, each of which weighs on average more than two tons, the most massive " oopart" object of our planet is in Egypt.
Originally the height of the Cheops pyramid was almost 150m, multiplied by a million

44

this gives us the distance Earth-
Sun (distance in meters). We also find there the
number pi, the exact calculation of the length of
a solar year, the exact calculation of the radius
and weight of the Earth, the law of precession of
the equinoxes, the value of the degree of
longitude, the actual direction of North.
The three pyramids are perfectly aligned by
relation to the stars of Orion's belt, and the
meridian of Giza divides the Earth in two
equal surfaces, hence the pyramid of Cheops
is also considered the navel of the
Earth, since it is located exactly on
its center of gravity. Forgotten Technology
attributed to ancient extinct civilizations?
Alien technologies? Time capsule? Or pure
chance? We still don't know why or
how they were built.

**In a show broadcast in the 70s
on TSR "les incollables", Jaques Bergier**
speaks about vanished civilizations. It relies on
extremely old and advanced civilized objects
on their time, exhibited in museums such as
Coso's object, or a magnetic oscillator found
frozen in a stone dating to a million years ago.
For Bergier these objects are irrefutable evidence
proving that Humanity has known several

civilizations technologically advanced having died out.

Jaques Bergier also evokes the theory of Von Däniken, who according to him could be one of the best hypotheses explaining the presence of these mysterious objects on Earth.

Indeed, several hypotheses can be made to try to explain the presence of these objects troublesome. Some of them like the pile of Baghdad or the map of the Ottoman Admiral Piri Reis can be explained by the recovery of technologies of very modern human civilizations advanced technologically and having died out, there thousands of years ago. But others cannot be explained and will be classified as "oopart" (out of place artifact).

Indeed, nothing allows us to explain these objects, they have no connection with the civilizations having coasted these lands and does not stick at all with the historical timeline. What drives us to Erich Von Däniken's hypothesis, is also the fact of that archeology does not allow us to observe a technological evolution, the older segments of the rock should include other objects technologically less advanced to gradually arrive at the object in question except this is not the case, the objects appear miraculously in the

middle of rock dated from 100 thousand, 500
thousand, 1 million or even billions of years. It is
that the hypothesis of a civilization having small
gradually progressed to reach a very high
level of technology to then turn off
can explain "oopart" objects. The only
logical hypothesis which almost imposes itself
naturally is that of civilizations
extraterrestrials who came to Earth in the very
retreated times, and have left behind them
technology far ahead of the indigenous.

I.7. Testimonies from Ancient to Contemporary age.

Our history is full of testimonies of flying objects. Here is a list of observations and anecdotes from Ancient to Contemporary age:

Ancient Greece:

The philosopher Anaxagon (-500 to -428), teacher of Pericles and Euripides, testifies having observed a considerable light and extraordinary the size of a large
beam which remained in place for several days. This description looks a lot like cigar-shaped spaceships that we can see nowadays.

India -329:

Alexander the Great crossing the river
Jaxartes witnesses two " shinning silver shields".
These flying objects would have dived on
his army disturbing the behavior of
horses and elephants. Which caused a big mess.
49

Ancient Rome. – 217:

In Capri, two shining shields in the sky and the
Moon fighting against the Sun.

In Capena, two moons showed themselves in full
day.

In Faléries, the sky opened and from this
opening a great light escaped.

Ancient Rome -103:

A burning torch furrowed the sky and at sunset
of the sun, a spherical body similar to a
shield was moving from West to East.

Shortly before the Battle of "Aix en Provence" at
"Amerie" and "Tuderte", we saw during the

night, the flaming javelins and shields that first
parted then fell against each other.
Finally, they all went towards sunset.

Ancient Rome -50:

Cicero delivers his famous speech:
"How many times has our senate not
asked with decemvirs to consult the oracles
when we have seen two suns and when three
moons appeared and flames of fires
were noticed in the sky; or, in this other
occasion, when the sun rose at night, when
noises were heard in the sky and the
cloud itself seemed to burst, and that one
strange globes, we noticed."

Ancient Rome -42:

In Rome, in the middle of the night a light shone
so strongly that the Romans rose up to
go about their daily tasks. The same year in
"Murtinum", local residents observed three
suns towards the third hour of the day, they
later came together to form one
single globe.

China 235:

A red meteor emitting sharp rays
fell from northwest to southwest on the
Liang camp. The meteor moved three
times back and forth over the camp, each
times of greater magnitude during its
forward movement and when withdrawing.

China 314:

Above the horizon, the Sun fell on the ground
and three other suns came out of it
Another day, the Sun quickly fell to the ground
and three other suns flew side by side, after
having risen to the West, they proceeded towards
the East.

Byzantium, Constantinople 436:

When the earthquakes followed at a frightening
pace, suddenly, and in the middle of a crowd of
people, a child was kidnapped by an unknown
force quite high in the sky so that we lose sight
of it; after which, being descended as he had
ascended, he declared to the
patriarch Procus, to the emperor himself and to
the people gathered, that he had just attended a
great concert of angels praising God.

Great Britain 457:

Over Great Britain and the North of
France, a flamboyant thing in the shape of
globe was seen in the sky. Its size was immense
and from this ball of fire issued two rays,
one which went further than France and the
other which went in the direction of Ireland, and
ended in fire, like beams.

France 584:

Saint Gregory, bishop of Tours, tells in
his Historia Francorum ("History of the Franks")
how, in 584, " bright rays of light that seemed to
intersect and collide, appeared in the sky "
and how, the following year, in
September, some people saw signs, namely rays
or domes as the ones we usually see spinning in
the sky".
Elsewhere, Saint Gregory describes "
golden globes" which, on several occasions, were
observed as they passed at
lightning speed in the sky of France.

France Meaux 729:

Monk Wilfred saw two large comets
revolving around the Sun...

France 760:

During the reign of Pepin the Short (715-768),
very strange phenomena appeared
publicly in France. The air was full of
human figures, the sky reflected mirages of
palaces, gardens, turbulent waves, ships the
sails in the wind and armies arrayed in battle.
The atmosphere was like a big dream.
We confused the dreams and the day before and
several people thought they were abducted by
aerial beings; madness struck the best of us and
the Church had to get involved. (Eliphas Levi
in "History of Magic").

Spain 827:

Eginard points out that during the expedition in
Spain of Pepin I, second son of Louis the Pious,
strange things happened: "truly this disaster was
preceded by terrible appearances of things in the
air". During the night they were sometimes pale
lights, sometimes fires bright and red as blood".

China 879:

One day there were two suns that fought
ardently. And another day of the same month,
two suns rose together and fought
in the sky, merging into a single star under
all the spectators.

Japan 900:

Vision of a burning wheel (heavenly wheel)
during the year 900, over Japan

Hungary 919:

A fiery torch and glowing spheres
like stars moved in the
Hungarian skies.

Japan August 3, 989:

The three objects shone slightly
ordinary and met at the same point of
their trajectory.

Switzerland 1104:

Wolffart notes that in Switzerland, in 1104, "bolts of fire, flying fire, were often observed in the sky that year; and they were close to the stars, like swarms of butterflies and little fiery worms of strange nature. They flew through the air and darkened the sun as clouds would have done.

England 1239:

In his "Historia Anglorum", British columnist Matthew of Paris writes:

"In 1239, as the sun of July 24 set down, a large torch-like star appeared above Hereford and Worcester (cities in the West of England, close to the border of Wales), the star rose up in the south to ascend into the sky giving great light. The star had the shape of a large head, the front part was sparkling and the back part was making smoke and lightning. The object turned to the North... neither fast nor slow, but precisely as if it wanted to go up to a place in the sky.

Great Britain 1290:

The Chronicle of William of Newburgh recounts how, at Byland Abbey in Yorkshire

(one of the largest Cistercian abbeys
of England), one day in 1290, then
the monks shared their meal, an "object
flat, round, silvery and shiny" flew over the
abbey, causing the greatest dread".

Great Britain Leicester 1388:

The Continuation of the Chronicle of Leicester,
by Henry Knighton, states that in November and
December 1388," a fire in the sky, like a
spinning and flaming wheel, or a barrel
circular of flames, emitting fire from above,
and others in the form of long fiery rays,
were observed in the winter in
the county of Leicester, and also in the county of
Northampton".

Burgundy, France 1461:

The Duke of Burgundy, in his memoirs,
recalls that on November 1, 1461 an object
appeared in the night sky, "long and wide
like half the moon, he remained without
move about a quarter of an hour, clearly
visible, then suddenly... it began to spin like
a spring and then fled into the heavens".

United States, Boston 1639:

James Everll saw a blazing light in the
sky. It was square or rectangular.
2.5 m to 3 m wide and moved in a zigzag.

Yuan, China 1639:

The villagers offered their condolences
to Yuan Yingta's family members,
Minister of National Defense during the
Ming Dynasty, who had sacrificed himself on the
battlefield by resisting the soldiers of the
Man. The villagers testify to having seen:
"We then saw a luminous thing in the form
star, red, white, yellow and blue, flying over the
funeral procession. This shiny thing did not land
on the ground, but it spun above the village for a
very long time, then went back up into the sky.
Its lights are seen up to more than five
kilometers away.

Wales 1692:

According to "Morden's Atlas of Wales": "a
fiery exhalation crossed the sea and set fire to
haystacks, wheat fields and
barns, very close to Harlech. This thing
infected the grass but it was not dangerous

57

for men, even for those who were close to it. It was happening always at nightfall, most often a Saturday or Sunday, and it lasted for some months. The only way to turn it off and scare it away was to sound a hunting horn or to fire gunshots..."

Ottoman Empire 1915:

We are in the Dardanelles during World War I, currently named çanakkale (Turkey). Allied forces attack the Ottoman Empire. The battle will last almost nine months and will make a total of half a million dead and will result in the victory of the Turks. In the English ranks 34000 dead will be listed and only 27,000 bodies will be found and identified. We have 7000 lost English soldiers and within these, 267 soldiers disappear in a very strange way.

We are August 12, 1915,
the English army, landed two days ago, fighting the soldiers of the Ottoman Sultan that shows him fierce resistance. The English soldiers could only advance 900 meters in 2 days.
It is in this context that the 267 soldiers of the 4th regiment of Norfolk, gone as scouts to invest a strategic hill begin their journey; and in the afternoon, ahead

the 22 New Zealand soldiers (engineers), the battalion of 267 soldiers begin their climb on the hill that a thick mist just covered. The cloud remains static until that the last of the soldiers enters it, and then gain height and move away advancing against the wind. 3 Of the 22 New Zealand soldiers, mentions this fact on their report. The soldier F.Reichard number: 4/165, private R.Nevnes 3/416 and Private J.L. Newman with no registration number.

On October 13, 1917, in Portugal, in Fatima.

In front of a crowd of more than 70,000 people, the rain stops, the clouds dissipate, revealing a shiny disc, mother-of-pearl color, which turns and emits rays of colored light. He stops to spin and fall to the ground with a movement of dead leaf fall, then it resumes its ascends and disappears into the Sun.
59

England, November 23, 1944:

Pilot Lieutenant Edward Schluter of the 415th Army Night Fighter Squadron of the American Air force based in England observes a real formation of about ten luminous discs moving at a high speed.

The training is followed on the ground
by Radarist Lt. Donald J. Meirs and aboard by
intelligence service lieutenant F.Ringwald,
(observer pilot).

I.8. UFO's crashes.

Some of these crashes are well documented,
press articles, photos, testimonials;
others unfortunately do not.
You will notice that between tries of military
prototype, bomb or device flywheel, meteorite,
hoax, and rumor; we didn't leave much room to
aliens.
The majority of UFO's incidents are of human
origin. The other cases are either explicable
natural phenomena or hoaxes.
Unexplained phenomena represent only a small
percentage and are not immediately attributable
to extraterrestrials.
Nevertheless 5 to 10% of them present
fairly convincing evidence, and could be
attributed to extraterrestrials.

1864 September, Cadotte, Missouri, USA.

Appeared October 30, 1865 in "The Cincinnati Commercial" "a messenger from the heavenly regions" and October 19, 1965 in "The Holy Louis Democrat" "A stone with engraved characters fall to the ground" Mr. James Lumley, an old trapper from the Mountains, declares to have seen above the Great Missouri Falls, a flying craft, shining and moving at very high speed eastward. Observation will last 5 seconds, after that the flying object will explode, according to Lumley like a flare. One roar followed by a violent wind, will leave him assuming that the flying object crashed.

The next day, the curious trapper will notice about 4 kilometers from his camp towards of the anomaly, that the ground was traced, the trees uprooted, razed hills and plowed land. He followed this path of disaster to discover at the end of it, a huge stone precipitated on the side of a mountain. He checked the fragments of the flying object scattered and found some of them had curious engraving like hieroglyphs.

The flying object is an authentic fact, because it was observed by neighboring cities, but no one found these famous stones engraved with hieroglyphs. Mr. Lumley may have embellished the anecdote or someone cleaned up afterwards its passage. This UFO has been classified as a comet.

June 6, 1884, Holdrege Nebraska.

The UFO crash will be published in the local newspaper "Nebraska Nugget" two days later as follows:
On June 6, 1884, a local rancher, John Ellis, and several other cowboys were participating in a roundup in rural Dundy County.
The cowboys heard a "sound of rumbling" in the sky. They looked up and saw a fiery and imposing object fall quickly on earth; after flying above their head, the object crashed into the ground in a ravine just beyond a hill. The men all approached cautiously, but the object was so hot, that a shepherd getting too close, was badly burned.
The men observed a strange kind of liquid hissing and bubbling on the ground while around the wreckage. Cogs, remnants of machines and pieces of metal were scattered everywhere, but everything was too hot to be approached. They brought back the man injured at Ellis' home to treat his burns, ready to come back the next day after the heat has subsided a bit. They described the

glow of the object as being almost as bright as the Sun. The cowboys came back the next day morning, this time with Police Inspector E.W. Rawlins. Rawlins took notes about what he observed there (including debris he closely inspected). The pieces of metal seemed similar to brass, but they were remarkably light. From the main wreck, Rawlins wrote in his diary:

"The Aircraft or whatever, seems to be about fifty or sixty feet long, cylindrical, and about ten or twelve feet in diameter".

A great excitement for the object arises in the neighborhood and the roundup is stopped. Everyone is waiting for the UFO to cool down, so they can take a closer look at it.

Mr. Ellis writes "In the afternoon, after the crash, a crowd of curious people gathered at the site of the crash to marvel at it and speculate about its origin.
Around 2 p.m., a huge storm broke out. The rain became more heavy and faster than anyone had ever seen. The wind shook off the rain and reduced the visibility to almost nothing. The storm lasted about 30 minutes before ending too abruptly that it had begun. And when

curious were able again to see the site of the crash, they were absolutely shocked. The mysterious object had disappeared.

PJ Nelson writes: "It has been said that the few small pieces that remained dissolved into ground. After the storm water were evacuated from the ravine, no trace of the debris was left".

Since the incident, this bizarre story has remade surface at least a few times. The first had place in the 1960s when a copy of the original newspaper article was discovered. Of the journalists and ufologists rushed the county of Dundy to interview local citizens and discover the whole story. But they were greeted with steely silence; no one wanted to talk about the story of the UFO crash. Interestingly, this Nebraska story seems to precede all other observations of UFOs reported in the newspapers of the time. Little Dundy County could very well be the **place where the UFO mania started so long ago.**

December 13, 1884, Sorisole, Bergamo, Italy.

Crash listed, information is
insufficient or from dubious sources.

April 17, 1897, Aurora, Texas, USA.

Possible hoax. Aurora Mayor Barbara
Brammer says that that year the crops
were bad, an epidemic and a great
fire hit the city. The inhabitants imagined
this scenario to draw attention to the city.

April 17, 1897, Leroy, Kansas, USA.

Possible hoax. One of the locals told everyone to
have seen an airship abduct one of his cows.

1907 Burlington, Vermont, USA.

Torpedo shaped UFO explodes above the
downtown Burlington, Vermont. Seen by
Bishop John S. Michaud, former governor
Alexander Woodbury, A.A. Buell and others.
This story is condensed from a report given in
the Burlington Free Press of June 3, 1907.
According to the story, several witnesses saw, a

strange ball of fire, enter the city with a large explosion, the object would have paused and remained in hovering and then dived., hitting a horse and stunning him momentarily. The object then has disappeared into the sky.
The object was described by a witness as being in the shape of a torpedo, six feet in length and about eight inches in diameter. He looked like burnished copper and would have emitted fire to several places on his body. Officials gave no explanation for the event. This flying object looks more like an army prototype than an alien craft.

June 30, 1908, Tunguska River, USSR.

An explosion, that releases an energy equivalent to a thousand times the Hiroshima nuclear bomb, destroyed the forest on a ray of 20 kilometers and does damage up to a hundred kilometers. The UFO has been listed as a meteor but some have put forward the hypothesis of a probable military test.

December 22, 1909 Chicago, Illinois, USA.

The UFO has been listed and observed by thousands of witnesses but the UFO's debris was never found.

1915 Puglia, Italy.

After a series of observations in 1915, following the crash of a UFO, a small green being would have been capture. No details, no report or even enough evidence.

1923 Quetta, Pakistan.

The crash has been listed but the information comes from dubious sources.

1925 Chevy Chase, Maryland, USA.

The crash has been listed but the information comes from dubious sources.

September 1925 Polson, Montana, USA.

The crash has been listed but the information comes from dubious sources.

1930 Mandurah, Western Australia.

A strange little entity is suddenly appeared at night in the ancestral home of Beryl Hickey, a small entity of one meter tall, bald, pink, with large

ears, a wide slit mouth without lips,
bulging eyes covered with a kind of film,
shiny skin as if greased, with
little hands and little erect pink feet
like those of a baby.
Beryl's father, who was very Christian, thought
that it was the devil and cast a net over this
creature, then dragged him outside.
We have no report on this story, only dubious
testimonies. The story is probably a rumor.

June 13, 1933 Italy Mussolini's Roswell.

A circular craft resembling a
pair of saucers joined at their edges
exteriors crashes near the town of Maderno, in
Lombardy, Northern Italy.

Description of the object:

The object, made of a thin silvery gray metal, is
approximately 15 meters in diameter and less
than 2 meters thick.
The double horizontal arms or the elements in
antenna shape are oriented in opposite directions
from a delta-shaped configuration surrounded by
a transparent blister. Two tubes are coupled
where the design tilts upward from a

flat underside, itself suspended with two other
pairs of oblong details.
Eleven portholes are visible in a straight line on
both side of the upper half of the aircraft.
Eight others portholes appear on its lower part,
always on both sides, but are interrupted
in the center of their line, on one side by a trio of
oval windows in what appears to be a
rectangular hatch. Six other windows or
ovoid lights, smaller and smaller, are
placed at each end of the aircraft, which
suffered damage during crushing.
No entities were discovered in this object

Several witnesses to the incident report it to
local authorities, who contact their superiors at
Milan for clear instructions.
The governmental authorities in Rome are
alerted and, in the hours that follow, top secret
orders are given.
By order of "Il Duce Benito Mussolini",
asking the authorities to "recover"
immediately the downed ship, to take it
in a safe place out of sight and to apply
strict censorship on any action related to the
crash.
After analysis, it turns out that the object is not
of this world. The technology it presents is

unknown and vastly superior to anything that was made on earth.

In 1938 Adolf Hitler and his scientists visited the hangar where the UFO was. The Nazis will strive to replicate the object from which their exceptional progress in the field of aeronautics during the Second World War. In 1945, before the arrival of the Allied troops, the hangar will be burned with the object.

1936 Black Forest, Germany, Freiburg.

The inhabitants of Freiburg **bear witness to a** huge crash in the dark forest. The Nazi army takes possession of the disc-shaped object. A dead alien would also be recovered. The reports of Nazi scientists attest to the work carried out on the object in particular to try to decipher the technology of the anti-gravitation.

1938 Czernica, current Poland. But belonging to Germany in 1938.

A flying disc crashed in a field (the field in question belonged to Eva Brown's parents) and was transported to the Hirschberg SS base by the NAZI army, then kept under high

surveillance. The disc was 7.6 meters in diameter and 3.8 meters high. It consisted of a large "crushing" dome, surrounded by an edge narrow exterior, and a smaller flat dome on the bottom with a flat bottom section.
The top of the dome was also flat and wide.
The craft had 6 oval-shaped structures resembling portholes but not transparent, where there were devices that radiated some type of light, located near the base of the dome superior.
3 entities were reportedly captured after the crash, here are their descriptions:

small dwarfs about 0.9-1.0 m tall, with large pear-shaped head, hairless heads of small bodies of dystrophic appearance, long narrow 4-fingered hands, grayish skin and large dark slant eyes.

1942 Los Angeles, USA.

During World War II, UFOs appear on radar, American military opened fire for several hours in the sky believing in a Japanese attack.
After the war, The Japanese military said it never sent a plane that way.

1941 Spring Cape Girardeau, Missouri,USA.

Reverend William Huffman is called by the local sheriff for giving the anointing to the wounded of the supposed plane crash. Once there, he finds a disc-shaped vessel. The device is broken and inside of it 2 aliens, one dead and the other suffocating. the Reverend testifies to having also seen hieroglyphs inside the object as well as a very futuristic control panel. The US Air Force cordons off the area, seizes the device and confiscates all evidence, photos, report and testimonials.

July 4, 1941, Tinian Island, Oceania.

The low-flying UFO was spotted by the Japanese air force. Three hunters chase him.
One of the hunters gets too close to the object and hit him. He still has time to warn its base of the presence of strange zeta-type silhouette. The UFO crashes into the ocean.
In 1944 the American army after having seized the island discovers the wreckage. The wreckage was classified as that of an exotic type spacecraft

1945 approximately near Great Britain.

The crash has been listed but the information comes from dubious sources.

1945 Mataquescuintla, Guatemala.

The crash has been listed but the information comes from dubious sources.

1946 Magdalena, New Mexico, USA.

Two children in search of a lost cow, see the crash. A saucer crushed on the side of a hill and inside the machine, creatures that can be described as small gray and fidgeting.

July 9 to October 15, Sweden.

Specifically, July 9 near the lake Barken, July 10 to Bjorkon, July 18 near of Lake Mjosa, on July 19 near Lake Kolmjarv, the August 16 in Malmo, mid-October Southern Sweden.

"Ghost Rockets" is the name given to mysterious objects in the shape of a rocket or missile that have been seen many times again in 1946, in Sweden. Military prototype attempt or alien technology? Here no crash but numerous observations, more than 2000 on a year.

January 1947 Papagos Indian Reservation, Aizona, USA.

Two former soldiers, while looking for a land to buy in the desert witness a cylindrical object half buried in sand and kept by soldiers.
Object description:
Domed disk; about 30 feet from diameter; two rings on its outer edge which seemed to have windows between them.

1947 May Spitsbergen, Norway.

Newspaper articles, "The Spitsbergen crash".

An accurate inspection of the flying disc, which was apparently controlled remotely and who had landed on the Nordaustlandet of Spitsbergen because of interference problems, led to The following indisputable information:

The flying object had a diameter of 48.88 m, and

slanted edges, was round and uninhabited.
The circular metal object is made of a
unknown metallic compound, looks like a
silver disc. After starting, 46
automatic escapements, located at
equal distances on the outer ring, make
spin the disc around a central ball
covered with plexiglass, containing
measuring and control equipment for the
remote control. Measuring instruments
have Russian symbols.
The radius of action of the disc seems to be
more of 30000 km, and the altitude of more than
160 km.
74

The flying object, which looks like one of the
legendary "flying saucers", has enough space to
carry powerful bombs, maybe even nuclear
bombs.

The Norwegian specialists assumed that the
disk had left the Soviet Union and was
fell over Spitzbergen due to a
transmission or reception error, and rendered
unusable due to hard landing.
The strange jet plane, unmanned and controlled
remotely, will be taken to Narvik on board a
vessel for further investigation.

After hearing the description of the disc,
Riedel, the designer of the German V weapon,
Said:

"It's a typical V-7, I personally worked on the
mass production of this model".

May 31, 1947 Socorro, New Mexico, USA.

Testimony of Sergeant Lonnie Zammora of the
Soccorro Police.

The sergeant left his car to help a UFO
immobilized in this quasi-desert region. The
object was observed by many tourists .
About 50 feet from the object, Zamora noticed
seeing a train landing gear and a red badge which
he then has drawn for the authorities. Zamora
then noted bright blue flames and a loud roar
until finally the object begins to move away from
its resting place.
After the incident, many local residents visited
the site and witnessed burned bushes and landing
gear failure. This incident was recorded in many
journals and articles and in many books and
magazines as well.

1947 July Near St. Joseph, Montana,

The crash has been listed but the information comes from dubious sources.

July 7-8, 1947 Roswell, USA.

July 7-8, 1947, MacBrazel a farmer finds strange debris in his field. Intrigued by these, he decides to show them to the owner from the neighboring farm. After that the events are linked, the sheriff of Roswell is advised of the facts, it alerts the nearest military base and a first press release is made by the Lieutenant Walter Haut. In this press release the lieutenant, spokesman for the military base of Roswell Army Air Field, says **"debris of a flying disc were recovered"**.
The next day, another press release will be made, contradicting and correcting the first **"the debris are not those of a flying disc but those of a sounding balloon"**. This statement leaves the first witnesses of the perplexed fact, for MacBrazel, his neighbor Loretta Proctor, the sheriff of Roswell and Major Jesse Marcel of the military Base of Roswell, the wreckage was really those of a UFO. One of the important points to mention on the testimonials, is the fact that no direct witness speaks of recovery

of extraterrestrial bodies. Witnesses
mentioning these, are indirect witnesses
who cite other witnesses who saw alien bodies.
The video of the alleged autopsy
of the extraterrestrial body attributed to one of
the extraterrestrials recovered from Roswell is
considered as a fake by almost all
ufologists.

The controversy over the recovery of
extraterrestrial bodies is not the most significant
event of the Roswell incident, a
multitudes of extraterrestrial bodies were already
collected in similar incidents. On the other hand
the hieroglyphic symbols engraved on the
debris, mentioned by direct witnesses, are
very disturbing. we find the same
symbols in some ancient Egyptian temples.
Translated, these hieroglyphs would symbolize
"the Stargate".

This subject deserves to be studied
much more seriously.

Finally, it is only around the 80s that the Roswell
affair remade surface. Until then, the Roswell
incident is a controversial UFO incident among
others and it is far from being the most
important. In 1978 the retired Major Jesse
Marcel claims in an interview that the debris
exposed to the press, one day after the incident,

were not those that they had found; and that the
authentic debris were those of a flying disc.

In 1980 the book "the Roswell incident" by
Charles Berlitz and William L. Moore based
largely on the testimony of Major Jesse
Marcel revives and gives momentum to
the Roswell affair which is considered a
important turning point in the history of ufology
but we find that, before and after this incident,
much more important facts have taken place.

July 5, 1947 Plains of San Augustin, New Mexico, USA.

Discovery of a disc-shaped device,
beached 240 km from Corona. The object was
undamaged and contained aliens inside.

July 31, 1947 Maury Island, Tacoma.

The crash has been listed but the information
comes from dubious sources.
Seems to be a prank.

August 13, 1947 Hopi Reservation, Arizona, USA.

Insufficient information. But a lot of

observations of a disc-shaped red flying object.

October 1947 Cave Creek, Arizona, USA.

Insufficient information. Observation of a red disc again.

1947 October 1947 Paradise Valley, Arizona, USA.

Many sightings. The red disc again

October 20, 1947 San Diego, California, USA.

The crash has been listed but the information comes from dubious sources.

1948 Kingman, Arizona, USA.

The crash has been listed but the information comes from dubious sources.

February 13, 1948 Aztec, New Mexico, USA.

The crash has been listed but the information comes from dubious sources.

1948 April 12, 1948 Near Aztec, New Mexico, USA.

The crash has been listed but the information comes from dubious sources.

March 25, 1948 Aztec, New Mexico, USA.

The crash has been listed but the information comes from dubious sources.

1948, March 25 White Sands, New Mexico USA.

The previous 4 dates seem to mention the same fact.

18 km north of Aztec, witnesses saw a disc-shaped object, 30 meters in diameter. The machine is commandeered by the army and transported to a secret base. There are many witnesses, press articles and book on this subject. Some even claim to have seen alien bodies.

On July 7/8, 1948, 38 miles from Laredo, Texas, USA.

A young Marine photographer, based in white Sands (New Mexico), is sent to mission to Laredo (Texas) to photograph the crash of a UFO 27 meters in diameter with its dead occupant.

August 19, 1949 Death Valley, California, USA.

Account of 2 prospectors, after a UFO crash, 2 living beings escape. Their story appears next day in the local press.

1950 Near Mexico City, Mexico.

Testimony of L. Ray. Dimmick an expert in explosive, after investigation nothing is found.

January 1950, Mojave Desert, California, USA.

Distorted version of the Newton/Gebauer's hoax.

February 18, 1950, Copenhagen, Denmark.

A couple of farmers see 2 saucers, one passes over the house, the second lands in the court of this one before exploding.

March 1950. Minnesota, New Germany, USA.

The FBI mentions the recovery of 3 saucers with 3 extraterrestrials on board. Seems to be a Newton and Gebauer's hoax.

1950 Birmingham, Alabama, USA. Sabab

The crash has been listed but only one witness speaks about it. Information insufficient.

April 1, 1950 Wiesbaden, Germany.

The crash has been listed but the information comes from dubious sources. Seems to be a April Fool.

April 1950 Argentina.

Observed by farmer Wilfredo H. Arevalo. Strangely, the alien's body disappeared the next day

May 10, 1950, Bahia Blanca Province, Argentina.

The crash has been listed but the information comes from dubious sources.

September 10, Albuquerque, Texas, USA.

After a UFO crash 3 alien bodies would have been recovered. We have no more information.

December 6, 1950, area of El Indio/Guerrero, Texas/Mexico border, Texas, USA.

TV documentary producer Jaime Shandera receives from an anonymous source a roll of undeveloped film containing what appears to be a government document that mentions both the Roswell UFO crash of 1947 and a "second" crash near El Indio-Guerrero. in 1950. Dated November 18, 1952, Eisenhower's briefing paper claims to have been written by Admiral Roscoe Hillenkoetter, the first director of the CIA, to brief new President Dwight Eisenhower from sponsored UFO investigations by the government. The document lists the

85

members of a top secret government committee on the UFO code named Majestic-12 who discusses U.S. efforts to conceal alien crashed and recovered spaceships in Roswell and in El Indio-Guerrero.

The facts:

On December 6, 1950, after following a long trajectory through the atmosphere, a second object, probably of similar origin to that of Roswell, slammed into the Earth at high speed in the El Indio - Guerrero area of the Texas border - Mexico.
When An investigation team arrived, what was left of the object had been almost completely incinerated. The salvageable materials were transported to the A.E.C. in Sandia, New Mexico, for study. »

1951 Sierra Madre, Mexico.

The crash has been listed but the information comes from dubious sources.
We have only one testimony and it is from an anonymous person.

In 1956, British ufologist Gordon Creighton reported in his magazine Flying

Saucer Review that according to J. Gonzalez Sanchez, FSR correspondent in Mexico, in Cuernavaco, in Mexico later in the summer of 1951, flying saucers appeared in a conversation between our special correspondent and the group of Mexican professionals. One of them, an engineer engaged in the construction of highways, said:

"I actually helped load a flying saucer and died crew in an American plane "Flying Box-Car", in an uninhabited valley in the Sierra Madre, near the workplace of his crew. "'Ah, Senior,' he said, 'they were beautiful, those little men, with handsome features and tiny beautifully shaped hands. But there must be to have had an explosion in their ship, because they were burnt black, and when I touched the face at one of them the skin came off under my finger as if it had been cooked! "We don't know anything else".

July 1952 Washington DC, USA.

From July 19 to 26. Many sightings, especially above the Capitol and near Washington National Airport.

July 23, 1952 Pueblo, Colorado, USA.

The crash has been listed but the information comes from dubious sources. Seems to be a prank.

August 1952, Ohio, USA.

The crash has been listed but the information comes from dubious sources.

August 15, 1952, Ely, Nevada USA.

After a UFO crash, **16 bodies are recovered.** This is the highest number of bodies found in the history of ufology. Yet the Ely crash goes almost unnoticed compared to Roswell and El indigo. The researchers have found some testimonials on the spot. A UFO crashes and the government cordons off the area. The next day, they announce that it was a plane of small size yet 12 witnesses affirm the opposite. No trace of the bodies. The story lack of evidence.

September 9, 1952, Spitsbergen, Norway.

Probable journalistic invention. The story appeared in German newspapers, she looks like

88

strangely to the crash of 1947.

1953 Brady, Montana USA.

The crash has been listed but the information comes from dubious sources. Army body retrieval, appears to be a tabloid invention.

April 18, 1953 Southwest Arizona, USA.

The crash has been listed but the information comes from dubious sources.

May 20, 1953 Western Utah, USA.

The crash has been listed but the information comes from dubious sources.

May 20/21, 1953 Kingman, Arizona, USA.

Several witnesses tell the same story, former servicemen and their children, their testimonials have been collected over several years and they all seem to fit together.

"The soldiers and scientists are taken to a UFO's crash site. They claim to have seen a flying disc sunk in 20 Cm of sand and their two occupants, measuring 4 feet approximately 120 Cm, they were decked out in silver jumpsuit.

June 19, 1953 Laredo, Texas, USA.

The crash has been listed but the information comes from dubious sources.
4 alien bodies would have been found.

1953 Camp Polk, Louisiana, USA.

After an accident, a saucer lands near Camp Polk, three aliens are moving away from the object. They will be captured dead and transported in a hangar in Washington D.C. Description from extraterrestrials:

Large helmeted heads, tight-fitting overalls, their legs were stiff, when they walked, 3.5 to 4.0 feet tall. (120cm high).

July 10, 1953 Johannesburg, South Africa South.

The crash has been listed and 5 extraterrestrial bodies have been found, but We don't know anything else.

October 13, 1953 Dutton, Montana, USA.

4 alien bodies recovered. Testimony of
Cecil Tenny, on vacation at Dutton. He observes
a smoke on the side of a mountain, being given
that forest fires are frequent in
the region, she pays no more attention to it.
The next day driving between Brady and Dutton,
she observes a flying object in the shape of a
cigar. The object flies low and is observed
by witnesses, apparently looking for the disc
steering wheel having crashed the day before.
After 7 minutes of observation, the object
accelerates and disappears.
The Montana State Police is notified.

Tenny stops by a bar and talks about her
observation. The same evening, he is called by
the Malmstrom AFB military base. The soldiers
ask him to come urgently to testify.
After doing her statement, she is accompanied to
the exit, it is during this journey, which she
observes officers wearing parcels with the
inscription "Top Secret". The
agents carrying the big bags and showing
signs of fatigue, drop one of the bags.
Cecil Tenny clearly sees a shape

91

Norse-like humanoid inside this one. After being garlanded, She is promptly fired.

1954 Mattydale, New York, USA.

In the suburbs of Syracuse, at 3 a clock, on a Sunday, a couple testified to having observed on the ground a 20-foot object examined by ground by men taking pictures. the
next day a police officer told them that this incident is a military secret.
Later the police will deny the incident.

1955 Eucla, Australia.

A newspaper says that 3 young people saw a UFO crashing and photographed his horned occupant.

May 5, 1955 Brighton, UK.

The crash has been listed but the information comes from dubious sources.
Seems to be a prank.

July 1955 Vestra Norrland, Sweden.

Very romantic invention of a tabloid of supermarket.

July 18, 1957 Carlsbad, New Mexico, USA.

The crash has been listed but the information comes from dubious sources.
4 bodies would have been found after this crash.

September 14, 1957 Ubatuba, Brazil.

A journalist from Rio de Janeiro, Ibrahim Sued, receives a letter from his readers. The letter is accompanied by a strange metal fragment from a UFO. The reader claims to have seen during part of catches a UFO exploding in front of him and his friends. The fragment was sent to the laboratory for analysis. We don't know anything else.

November 21, 1957 Reasty Hill, Scarborough, Yorkshire, UK.

The crash has been listed but the information comes from dubious sources.

1958/1959 Woomera, Australia.

The information is insufficient to prove anything about an alleged crash of UFO. But the military nuclear test base of Woomera, also called Area 53, is regularly subject to missile tests. Of the UFO testimonies are not rare there.

1958 Utah Desert, USA.

The crash has been listed but the information comes from dubious sources.

1958 North of Rome, Italy.

An entire neighborhood suffers a power outage and some residents claim to have seen a UFO.

January 21, 1959 Gdynia, Poland.

Gdynia dockers and port guards, observe, the night of January 21, a luminous object falling right in the middle of the harbor basin.

The day after divers go up, they believed a few metal parts belonged to the UFO.
A being six feet tall with a strange combination wandering on the beach and at half burned is captured and transported to the hospital.
After examination the doctors notice that these organs are different from those of humans, the humanoid creature has 6 fingers and 6 toes. He

would have lived until a doctor took him away a kind of armband. The creature was then requisitioned by the Russian military.

September 17, 1959 Amsterdam Wormer.

The crash has been listed but the information comes from dubious sources.

1960 Spain.

The crash has been listed but the information comes from dubious sources.

1960 Great Sand dune, Colorado, USA.

The crash has been listed but the information comes from dubious sources.

March 1960 New York USA Paltz.

Witnesses reported that a small humanoid had been found near his flying machine while that his two co-pilots were escaping. The alien was in the care of the C.I.A and died at 28 days later.

1961 Lubeck, Germany.

A former NATO testifies to come across on a
top-secret file, entitled "cosmic
top-secret", here is his testimony:

[Dean talks about the secret file which he claims
to have seen on a desk at NATO.]
"The appendix that really shocked me was called
"Autopsy". I've seen pictures of a 30 meters disc
that crashed in Timmensdorfer, Germany, near
of the Baltic Sea in 1961.
The British army, according to the report, arrived
first and prohibited the access of the
perimeter. The craft had landed near the Russian
border and had not been destroyed, but a third
of it was buried. The Russians and us, detected
the aircraft.
Inside, there were 12 small bodies, all of them
dead. In the secret file, there are photos of these
beings known as 'gray,' beings were exposed and
then loaded in jeeps.

There were also autopsy's photos.
According to the report of the expert, the grays
seemed had been made in the same mold -
clones without digestive system, some of the
little grays seemed not to be species capable of
reproduction. They didn't have urinary system.

The aircraft was cut six-piece crust, put on trucks to taken away. Rumor has it that, the aircraft was given to the Americans and flown to the Wright-Patterson Air Force, military Base in Ohio. I looked at these pictures and I couldn't believe it. I got goosebumps and thought, "My God, I never really believed that we were alone in the universe, but he was hard to swallow that!"

April 28, 1961, Lake Onega, USSR.

The crash has been listed but the information comes from dubious sources.

April 18, 1962, Las Vegas USA.

The observation begins in New York and makes thousands of witnesses. The extremely luminous object is mistaken for a meteor. The UFO lands in Eureka, causing a power outage in the city, and takes off from Eureka to go to Las Vegas, where witnesses observe it crashed inside the military complex of Nellis.

July 16, 1963 Chalton, Wiltshire UK.

The crash has been listed but the information comes from dubious sources.

December 10, 1963 Cosford UK.

According to various sources, on December 10,
1963, two members of the Royal Air Force
observed a strange dome-shaped flying object in
his fall behind an RAF base hangar
of Cosford, near Wolverhampton, in
England.
Both soldiers said the craft had
scanned the airfield with strange green ray light.
When the soldiers come to help any survivors,
the object was no longer there.
After an investigation the case is classified top-
secret.
A few days later, a very large cargo aircraft lands
on the base, which is unusual for
this base, and a large camouflaged object was
loaded

December 10, 1964 Fort Riley, Kansas USA.

A senior military base officer at Fort
Riley gives the order to 4 soldiers, who are on
guard tonight, to guard a place. Once on site,
the soldiers notice that a perimeter of
security has already been placed by the army and
a military helicopter projecting its beacon of
tracking on a landed disc-shaped object

on the ground. Soldiers testify that the 12m object long and 5m wide, was evacuated the following day on a trailer truck. Some ufologists claim that 9 dead aliens would have also been on the trip.

January 1965 San Miguel, Argentina.

Near the Andes, residents observe a UFO crashing in San Rafael. A small humanoid with phosphorescent diving suit is also observed alongside the craft. The Argentinian army has taken possession of the object.

December 9, 1965 Kecsburg Pennsylvania USA.

A gigantic fireball observed on 5 States and by thousands of witnesses crashes to Kecsburg, some speak of meteors others of UFO. The army requisitioned the object.

1967 Missouri USA.

A certain gentleman "Loftin" would have found a 1m disc and handed it over to "USA Testing Company".

December 6, 1967, Shag Harbour, Canada.

Testimony of Laurie Wickens, four of her friends. The group of friends drive through the city from Shag Harbor at 11 p.m, when a large object (about twenty meters in diameter according to witnesses) crosses the sky in front of them. The various witnesses describe an object in the shape of a "bowl", of "amber" color, carrying four lights that flash in sequence and following a downward trajectory of about 45 °. Quickly, the object ends its course in the waters of the port, producing a luminous "flash", as well as a large sound explosion, before sinking.

The day after the divers meticulously scrutinize the place of the incident but finds no trace of the UFO.

February 12, 1968 Orocue Colombia.

The inhabitants note three explosions, shortly after seeing a flying object in the shape of disk. As the result of an investigation carried out by military, debris is found. Sent to Bogota, a American attaché first declares that these are the debris from a spaceship, then later statements suggest that it comes from of the entry of an American satellite into the atmosphere.

March 25, 1968, Nepal. India. Bhutan.

After a series of sightings, a total of 6 UFOs, from March 4 to February 21. According to the report of the CIA. "A metallic disc-shaped object with a base of 180 cm and 120 cm in height was found in a crater at Baltichaur, five miles NE of Pokhara.

1971 Edwards Air Force base.

A quick reminder, this base is the place where the president Eisenhower spoke in 1954 with the representatives of two extraterrestrial races.

A summer night, Debbie Clayton hears an object crash into his property. She starts walking towards it joined by other residents. A once there, observes a cloud dissipates and behind him, a mushroom-shaped UFO with flashing green lights. HAS inside the device three gray humanoids and a human woman in a pink jumpsuit tight-fitting. they were all still alive.
The army arrives very quickly on the spot, closes the perimeter, and asks local residents to leave the premises. The UFO will be transported to Edwards Army Base.

January 23, 1974, Wales.

Seismic light after an earthquake
of magnitude 3.5 interpreted by local residents
like a UFO crash.

May 1974 AFB Germany, Ramstein.

A UFO is shot down by an American air missile.
The disc-shaped object heavily damaged is then
sent to the United States for analysis. aliens from
type "grey dwarf" died during accident, but their
number is unknown.
The device was listed as a typical aircraft of the
zeta-reticular-system.

May 17, 1974, Chile.

A UFO is transported from an impact zone to
Kirtland Army Base.

August 25, 1974, Chihuahua, Mexico.

Collusion between a UFO and a small plane. the
UFO would have been towed, followed by
military censorship. After investigation, it turns
out that it was the crash of a "Cessna" aircraft

involved in a drugs traffic that the army towed away?

May 12, 1976 Desert, Australia.

After a UFO crashed in the desert, four extraterrestrial bodies are recovered. We don't know anything else.

April 5, 1977 South West Ohio, USA.

After the crash of a UFO, 11 extraterrestrial bodies are recovered. No further information.

June 22, 1977 Northwestern Arizona, USA.

After the crash of a UFO, 5 extraterrestrial bodies are retrieved, no further information.

August 17, 1977 Tobasco, Mexico.

After the crash of a UFO, 2 extraterrestrial bodies are recovered. No further information.

1978, Lake Ul'ken-Borly, Kustanay region, Kazakhstan.

The army recovers an alien body of the type "small grey" and its flying disc. only one testimony of Anton Belousov.

1978, Ocean of Finland.

After a collision between a Russian fighter plane and a UFO. The UFO crashes into the ocean and is recovered by the Russian army as well as these occupants.

May 6, 1978 Padcaya, Bolivia.

A disc-shaped flying object crashes into the side of a mountain. The army organizes a shipping but following the bad atmospheric conditions returns empty-handed.

1982 China, Gobi Desert.

The Army recovers a crashed and deserted UFO by its occupants in the Gobi Desert. Seems be a prank.

1988 Russia Dalnegorsk or Hill 611.

Residents of the city of Dalnegorsk watch
a large reddish flying disc, flying very low
arrived at the level of hill 611, it crashes.
The debris is recovered and analyzed,
conclusion: alien craft.

November 1988 Afghanistan.

During the Afghan war 1979-1989,
the Russian army recovers a disc object as well as
7 alien bodies.

November 20, 1989, Canada, Quebec, Maryville.

After a series of strange light sightings
for 2 days. A perfect disc-shaped aircraft is found
in the property of one of the witnesses.

May 7, 1989 Kalahari Desert, Botswana, South Africa.

The facts are disputed.
A UFO is shot down by 2 mirages belonging to
the South African Air Force. He crashes into the
desert of Kalahari. Item description: 18m
in diameter, 9m in height and weighing 50 tons.

2 living humanoid beings of "small gray type" are recovered. Everything will be sent to the USA.

September 27, 1989 Voronezh, Russia.

According to a group of children, a UFO lands in a park. A robot and a terrifying creature come out of the device.
They try to kidnap the children, pointing a bright light at one of the children, the child disappears and reappears after five minutes. Finally, the robot and the creature enter in their ship and flee. The story is unreliable for authorities and ufologists.

September 28 Smith's Point Beach, Long Island, New York, USA.

Observed by many witnesses, a intervention in which 6 helicopters, 4 of the army and 2 of the Suffolk police are involved against 2 huge triangular objects.
The helicopters circle one of the objects, while that the second shot down, crashes on the beach.
The places are secure and the beach will be closed very long time. They are many witnesses and photos of this intervention. (Source: LIUFON)

106

September 2, 1990 Megas Platanos, Greece.

Witnesses claim to have seen the night of 2 September, 12 to 17 UFOs flying over the region of Peloponnese to central Greece. Close to village of Megas Platanos, local residents hear explosions after observing the same objects. One of them crashes not far from the village but the place is inaccessible at night. The morning the local residents arrive on site and villagers can observe traces of the explosion but no trace of the flying object.

But October 19, 1990 armed her Greek Air Force, its research and development department makes a statement, the military concludes that the debris collected was of terrestrial origin.

April 15, 1992 Niagara Falls, USA.

A disc-shaped object crashes into the road 270. It is 8m high and 30 in diameter. The authorities are very quickly on the spot, they evacuate the object and clean the place.

November 1992 Long Island, New York, USA. Southaven Park, Shirley.

Videos, photos and testimonials leaked by a group of local investigators on a bright reddish object having crashed at Southaven park.

January 20, 1996 Varginha, Brazil.

Capture of aliens by the army following a crash. A UFO crashes violently near the town of Varginha. The army, the police and the fire brigade quickly secure the crash site and evacuate the object. There are many witnesses.
The following days, other witnesses claimed having seen extraterrestrial entities attempting to hide in town.
A real hunt starts to capture the aliens.
Some are captured, others killed and wounded. One of them will even be autopsied at the hospital of the city. The aliens will then be transported to the Albrook base in Panama.
A year later 15 witnesses agree to talk about it, one of them even affirms that we would have tried to buy his silence.

August 27, 2000 Balochistan.

Observation of 6 or 7 flying rockets or missiles
at very high speed over Quetta and others
cities of Balochistan. No data on
the place of landing or a possible crash of
the objects.

November 2006 Bahia, Brazil.

A flying saucer seen on a truck,
probably just an industrial part.

May 27, 2008 Phu Quoc, Vietnam.

The media talk about UFOs, probably to design
a fighter jet. The plane indeed corresponds to the
description of unidentified flying object,
probably a plane carrying out a secret mission,
after its crash, no country claims it. After analysis
of the debris, the authorities note that it is well
and truly airplane but his origin is unknow. And
because no country claims it, the object becomes
a UFO.

This example illustrates how the
terminology for UFO has evolved, nowadays it
no longer indicates an outgoing event of

109

the ordinary and involving extraterrestrials.
A new term tries to replace it, U.A.P. to say
"Unidentified aerial phenomena".

Conclusion, what can we deduce from these
crashes or sightings? After eliminating all
doubtful cases. We have 10 to 15% of cases left
well documented that allow us to deduce
that:

Before and during World War II,
NAZI Germany seems to have recovered this
alien technology. They multiply the
disc-shaped prototype tests. The
many crashes and UFO sightings occurred in
their area of influence during this period of
history attests to this. After the
Second World War. NAZI technology
passes into the hands of the Americans with the
"Operation Paperclip" but above all in the
hands of the Russians, real victor of the second
world war. Most UFO crashes will be
after the war observed in the United States and
the USSR. The two world powers are testing
their disc-shaped prototypes using awkwardly
from the antigravity technology, we can see this
in the many accidents that occurred during this
period. Most were not of extraterrestrial origin.
There are many cases in the United States where

the pilots of these machines, damaged after a landing or crash, repaired the prototypes sometimes even in front of residents.

After Hiroshima and Nagasaki, the UFOs of extraterrestrial origin are multiplying and the Roswell incident is a big turning point for ufology, although similar cases are recorded before and after this one.

Begins after Roswell the nuclear testing period, and with it, a great misinformation project around the subject of UFOs of extraterrestrial origins, known as "Blue Book Project".

Currently, UFO sightings and accidents of extraterrestrial origin are on the rise and at the same time the media machine is working hard to suppress or discredit these facts.

I.9. The UFO sightings.

Compared to crashes, UFO sightings
reported are much more numerous and
growth every year. We speak of "reported
observations" because many of them
they often are not. The growth
of these observations is also due to the
improvement of our technology.
Indeed, if we compare the
number of people equipped with a camera, in the
50s compared to 2020, it is normal that we have
a lot more videos and photos today. Let's base
us on the figures of the SOBEPS (Société belge
d'étude des phénomènes spatiaux, "Belgian
society for the study of space phenomena")

According to figures from SOBEPS, there is on average in Belgium, which is a very small country compared in the United States, 100 UFO phenomena in the Belgian sky per year; with a sighting record in 2018. In 2018, SOBEPS identified 255 observations. Now take the numbers of the UN since 1947, we have no less than 150 million reported observations identified in the world. Knowing that only 5 to 15% of people witnessing UFO sightings contact the authorities, it is not difficult to imagine that the true number of observations should be over a billion. According to SOBEPS and other ufologists, after filtering serious, only 5% of these observations remain unexplained. Let's take back our billion observations since 1947, 5% of one billion makes us 50 million unexplained sightings; And if we take the figures from the UN, 5% from 150 million, brings us to 7.5 million unexplained sightings. So that makes us a lot of unexplained.

List all these sightings since 1947, doesn't really matter here. But we have to point out that the UFO frequency is increasing before and after every natural disaster. Through example before and after the earthquake from 1999 in Turkey in the Marmara region

which left 17,480 dead and 10 thousand missing
or again during the 2004 tsunami or the number
missing is 250,000.

UFOs are also particularly active at
around military bases, among others, before
and after nuclear tests.

Unfortunately, these sightings are not
studied as they should and after
some headlines to entertain people, they
they are quickly forgotten.

We will analyze three types of sightings.
The first two demonstrate that these beings exist
and are benevolent towards us.
The third demonstrates that "UFOs" does not
immediately mean extraterrestrial

1. Chelyabinsk Meteor.

February 15, 2013, Chelyabinsk, Russia.
A meteor 17 meters in diameter and a
mass of 10,000 tons enters the atmosphere
and heads towards the city of Chelyabinsk and
the meteor explodes in the sky without
apparent reason.

The phenomenon is filmed by many

witnesses. Watch in slow motion, we can clearly observe a small round light approaching the meteor and moving away from it afterwards blewing it up. The UFO also takes a opposite trajectory compared to the fragments of the exploded meteor. The video is analyzed by world's scientists and ufologists and they find no trickery there. In the press also, the phenomenon produces as at the usual a few headlines, before drown in the mass media pollution, that is wrongly called information. 7 years after here is what we can read on Wikipedia.

**This is a copy paste from the Wikipedia page
dealing with the subject:**

he Chelyabinsk meteor was a superbolide that entered Earth's atmosphere over the southern Ural region in Russia on 15 February 2013 at about 09:20 YEKT (03:20 UTC). It was caused by an approximately 20 m (66 ft) near-Earth asteroid that entered the atmosphere at a shallow 18.3 ± 0.4 degree angle with a speed relative to Earth of 19.16 ± 0.15 kilometres per second (69,000 km/h or 42,690 mph).[6][7] The light from the meteor was briefly brighter than the

Sun, visible as far as 100 km (62 mi) away. It was observed in a wide area of the region and in neighbouring republics. Some eyewitnesses also said they felt intense heat from the fireball.

The object exploded in a meteor air burst over Chelyabinsk Oblast, at a height of about 29.7 km (18.5 mi; 97,000 ft).[7][8] The explosion generated a bright flash, producing a hot cloud of dust and gas that penetrated to 26.2 km (16.3 mi), and many surviving small fragmentary meteorites...

The text from "Wikipedia" spans several pages and you can read and see that our UFO is not mentioned anywhere in this article. the meteor would have fragmented for no reason apparent at an altitude of 40 km. I invite you to watch the video, you will see that the meteor is exploded, you will also hear three detonations.
It's sad how the information is distorted, while the major event of this phenomenon should be, this flying object having by his heroic intervention saved thousands of humans, his intervention here is not unfortunately not mentioned, officially

it therefore did not take place.
So pushing the reflection further, we
are entitled to ask ourselves if the meteor
was not detonated by an earthly military
mechanism. The rest of the article denies this
hypothesis.

Wikipedia:

**"The bolide was not detected before starting
its atmospheric entry. Several programs
detection of asteroids whose orbit
carries a risk of collision with the Earth
have been implemented from the end of the
years 1990, notably by NASA. But this
research, difficult to carry out given the
size of objects and their low albedo, cannot
detect only the largest asteroids and
therefore presenting a much greater risk:
asteroids with a diameter greater than
kilometer are searched systematic, while the
detection of asteroids with a generally larger
diameter at 100 meters remains random.
Moreover, this object relatively small
seemed to come from the depths from the
east, as then seen from the earth's surface:
its trajectory was thus veiled by the glare
of the rising Sun, which prevented any
detection early [4]. »**

We can see that the authorities have
not detected the meteor before it entered
the earth's atmosphere and no strategy has been
designed to counter it. Another reason to
ignore the heroic UFO's intervention.

2. Deactivation of nuclear missiles.

In the sixties, we are in "cold war". Both blocks
are in the arms race. United States
chained nuclear missile tests.
Lieutenant Robert Salas testifies to the facts.
March 6, 1967, Malmstrom Montana military
base belonging to the U.S. Airforce:

A red oval-shaped flying object disables
one by one, the ten intercontinental nuclear
ballistic missiles.

The same phenomenon occurred on March 24,
1967 on the Oscar Fight military base.

Lieutenant Robert Jacobs responsible for
photographing each missile fire, testifies that
September 15, 1964, military base of
Vandenberg, a red flying saucer,
intercepts by firing four laser beams at a

missile fired from the military base and flying at 8000 km/h; the missile is disabled.

A day later Robert Jacobs is summoned by Major Florenz J. Mansmann. The movie is projected and the major stops the projection and asks to Jacobs, "what is that?". Jacobs responds, "It looks like a UFO". The major resumes, " You keep it to yourself, it never happened". After that, they made Lt. Jacobs swear to keep quiet.

These examples illustrate the character benevolent aliens towards us, and how this information is concealed from General public.

3. The Belgian UFO's wave.

Belgium, Brussels on November 29, 1989, a few weeks after the fall of the wall of Berlin. This period beginning at the end of 1989 and ending around the summer of 1991, will enter literature as "the Belgian UFOs wave". I was seven years old, and I was sleeping on a bed superimposed, on the back floor of our house of two floors, with my older brother. Our bedroom had a very large attic window giving on a large garden. There was no building, trees or other obstacles likely to obstruct

the view of the stars. I often observed the
reflection moonlight on the wall facing
the large window before I fell asleep, and
strangely that night, we didn't have a
but two luminous reflections. The first on
the right end of the wall and the second on
the left end. Astonished and with the naivety of a
seven-year-old child, I told my big brother,
**well it's weird, tonight we have two
moons!"**. My brother neither paid any attention,
retorting that I had better try to sleep.
But as I insisted, he ended up giving in to my
whims and got up to observe the anomaly. And
there, bad luck for him, the two balls
white lights to which a third
added, changed places. my two moons
had become three and were rotating. That
looked like a compound propulsion engine
of three giant lighthouses rotating around a
central axis. We used to see this kind
of engine on the spaceships of the Hollywood's
films. My brother, impressed, fell
on his back. After this anomaly, we
rushed to the window, but the flying object
disappeared.

The next day, the country was shaken. The
media only talked about this phenomenon,
SOBEPS, Belgian Space Phenomena Society, had

collected 143 testimonies. The UFO had been observed in Brussels, but especially in the region border with Germany, in Verviers and Eupen. Apparently other people had been luckier than us because they had been able to observe the UFO very closely. Here are their testimonials:

Two gendarmes (Nicollet and Von Montigny) patrolling that night in the heights of Eupen, explain the anomaly:

We saw big headlights below a machine that we did not know how to describe, and the floor was really lit. We could have read the newspaper there. I saw a triangle, three headlights and a blinking ball crawls. While we observed this one, suddenly from behind the trees popped the other gear. Same lighting power but with a rapidity, as if it had been catapulted. Everyone was listening to our radio. Some had laughing. They thought of Santa Claus. They were scared like us.

Dieter Plumans, retired gendarme of the Calamine testifies:

- If I remember correctly, we had already seen Something. The "gendarmes" patrol had took the road to "Henri-Chapelle" then stopped

in front of a silent and static UFO, just
above a nursing home. The two
"gendarmes" kept their cool a few minutes then
the UFO disappeared into the sky.

Here is one of the 143 testimonies collected by
the SOBEPS:

- let's say it was huge and it had the shape
of a triangle. I went to the window to
see and I saw all these little lights, like
stars.

After these testimonies, the President of the
SOBEPS concludes:

"- These are not laser beams and again
less holograms. It is obviously a
material and solid object that has moved in
space."

Steven Spielberg's E.T. movie was very
popular, and we were living our own alien story.
After that day everything became possible. For
almost three years, more than 200
observations will be made in Belgium.
We felt at the advent of an incredible event,
which was bound to happen (meeting with an

extraterrestrial civilization) because the frequency of UFO sightings broke records.

But nothing happens; nothing occurs because what we observed was the plane ASTRA TR3b or XRZ. A antigravity aircraft with magnetohydrodynamic propulsion, of triangular shape. The triangular machine with futuristic curves used the magnetic force of the Earth, was surprisingly quiet and could move at no more Mac10, no more no less than a prototype of the US Army. There was no alien, unfortunately, but only human technology, far ahead of its time. Even though, it must be admitted that some extraterrestrial UFOs could have taken the wave.

It is for this reason that the Belgian UFO wave is not sufficient evidence of the existence of extraterrestrials, but this is a very good example to prove that a UFO should not be automatically equated with extraterrestrial.

I.10. Blue book Vs Disclosure.

On July 16, 1945, the US army detonates the first
nuclear bomb of the world at the Trinity site,
located thirty kilometers southeast of San
Antonio, New Mexico. Three weeks later, on
August 6 and 9, the United States ended
the Second World War. using the
bomb to destroy Japanese cities
from Hiroshima and Nagasaki. This produces a
multiplication of UFO's cases, UFO crashes and
recovery of alien bodies in the USA. Sightings
and crashes are so many, that they begin to
worry the authorities. The San Antonio incident
at the New Mexico, where the army recovers a
UFO having crushed, more or less in the same
place where the nuclear test had taken place a
month ago, rather alarm them.

The NSA will call on two scientists from
Renowned, physicist Robert Oppenheimer of
Princeton University, also known as the father
of the atomic bomb, and Albert Einstein; to
a top-secret classified report in which the NSA
request to analyze whether the increase in UFOs
in the American sky correlates with the
nuclear tests?

One detail is strange in the conclusions of this
Report, presented in June 1947, authorities and
other stakeholders seem to be very comfortable
with the fact that aliens exist
It is in this report that the term EBE
"Extraterrestrial Biological
Entities" is used for the first time.

Two scientists raise several problems
what the extraterrestrials might pose. They go
even so far as to claim that extraterrestrials
would have the right to have our earthly colony;
citing as an example the regimes of
mandates established after the first
world war. The final conclusion of the report is
very striking.

Oppenheimer and Einstein conclude:

" We declare that extraterrestrial entities exist and have been visiting Earth for thousands of years".

One of the questions in the report concerns the disclosure of this information to the general public. Scientists answer it like this:

"If you disclose this information without at beforehand organize the repercussions that this could have on society, the law, the finance and religions, the world could be plunged into chaos"

In the history of ufology, 1947 is very important a turning point. It is after this date that the concealment policy begins or rather is accentuated. All UFO incidents will be treated in the top-secret register, and "the citizens' right to information" will be flouted. It is also after this date we observe the division of the world into two zones of influence for the recovery of debris or extraterrestrial entities, probably due to the Cold War. As the "Treaty of Tordesillas" between the Kingdom of Castile and Portugal, the U.S.S.R. and the

126

USA divides the world in two. Thereby debris from an incident that occurred, for example, at Peru will be shipped to the United States while that those recovered in Poland will go to The U.S.S.R.

It's in this context that the U.S Air Force. put in place in 1947, a commission to charge to investigate the UFO phenomenon, entitled "Sign". Then, in the same vein, the project "Grudge" will succeed him 1948-1952, to finally arrival at the project "Blue Book" 1952-1969.

The official objectives of the "Blue Book" project are:

1. Find an explanation for all of the testimonials of UFO sightings.

2. Determine if UFOs represent a threat to the security of the United States.

3. Determine if UFOs exhibit a advanced technology compared to progress of the United States and whether this could be exploited.

Unfortunately, the commission will never be honest in his dealings. The "Blue Book project"

will be responsible for discrediting all
UFO testimonies and ridicule in the
media anyone claiming that the UFO
phenomenon would be of extraterrestrial origin.
In front of this arrogant and closed attitude of
the military and some scientists who are part of
the project, even the professor astronomer
ufologist, Josef Allen Hynek who was part of the
project since "Sign" 1948, and great skeptic
of the UFO phenomenon, will change his
opinion.
When asked, what had done to him
change his mind, he replied:

"Two things, actually, the first was the attitude
completely closed from the Air Force. They
didn't give UFOs a chance to exist, even if they
were flying over a street in the middle of the day.
Everything had to have an explanation. I was
starting to get on my nerves, even though I
originally felt the same as them, I knew now that
they were off track.
You can't assume a thing doesn't exist
not if you don't have proof. Secondly,
the quality of the witnesses began to trouble me.
A few cases have, for example, been reported by
military pilots, and I knew they had been
well trained, so this is where for the first time

times I thought maybe there was something behind it all".

And for the scientific part of the project, it declared:

"As a scientist, I must be aware of the past, too often, subjects of great scientific importance have been neglected because the new phenomenon was out of the scientist norm of the time."

He will also write in 1968 a furious letter addressed to Colonel Raymond S. Sleeper, one of the responsible for the project, in which he deplores, among other things, the lack of resources allocated to investigators, the botched investigations and the lack of consideration given to witnesses.

Here is a passage:

"It would be appropriate for the US Air Force to admit that the UFO phenomenon is a problem world-class scientist who can have a great impact"

Finally, the "Blue book" project came to an end in 1969 with the Condon report. Report commissioned by US. Aire Force to Professor Edward Condon of the University of Colorado. The report supposed to be neutral after studying 56 cases of the "Blue book project" and all the cases of the period 1968-1969, concluded that these phenomena were due to the misinterpretation of natural phenomenon, that they could bring nothing in terms of new technology to the army, and that they bring nothing to the probably existence of aliens.

So many sightings, crashes, testimonials, extraterrestrials body recovery sometimes even in front of witnesses, were only the fruit of a collective paranoia and a fad. It is on these conclusions that officially the "Blue book" project ends.
But unofficially the program of misinformation continues under the name of the project "Aquarius".
Meanwhile the subject is picked up by the tabloids, which discredits all new serious initiatives, and of course we can't count on the collective hypocrisy of the mass media to give us quality information on the subject.

I wonder what happened between the
Oppenheimer and Einstein report of June 1947
in which, aliens are a no-brainer
and Edwards Condon's 1969 report, where they
become almost an invention of paranoia
collective.

The counter-attack of the ufologists will arrive
belatedly, on May 9, 2001, with the project
"Disclosure" by ufologist Steven M. Greer who
will bring together an impressive number of
documents, testimonials, videos and photos to
force the authorities into a public disclosure.
It should also be noted that in the United States,
the subject is taken
more seriously than in Europe. She is almost at
each campaign for the presidency, a
electoral promise of one of the candidates. The
latest being Bernies Sanders and Hillary
Clinton. In this context the initiative of Steven
Mr. Greer doesn't seem so far-fetched.

Here is a summary of the project conference
"Disclosure" of May 9, 2001.

On Wednesday, May 9, 2001, the project was
presented to the public and media at the
National Press Club (Washington, D.C.).

The conference begins with an introduction of actor Jon Cypher who paraphrases the slogan from the X-Files series "the truth is out here" in claiming: "The truth is here!"

Geer then took the floor thanking Sarah McClendon (White House correspondent for McClendon News Service) for its support, then asserting, among other things, that the US and British governments have long had secret exchanges with extraterrestrials, that they would hide from humanity the existence of a new energy capable of replacing oil, solving environmental problems related to the overexploitation of hydrocarbons and the greenhouse effect.

Then a series of people deliver their testimony, indicating to wish to be able to redo in detail during an official hearing of the Congress:

John Callahan (FAA Divisional Office Manager, Accident and Investigation) on Japan Air Lines aeronautical observation;

Charles Brown (lieutenant-colonel of the AFOSI in retirement) who participated in Project Grudge;

132

Michael Smith (air traffic controller sergeant of USAF);

Graham Bethune (Pilot, Commanding Officer retirement from the US Navy) on the observation of Gander;

Dan Willis (US Navy), who will say he received a message from a ship that observed an object leaving the sea.

A dozen witnesses from the US Army, officials from federal agencies and bodies such as the Direction of the International Civil Aviation Organization.

Don Phillips of Lockheed Skunkworks (sub-dealing with the CIA), suggesting that the pilots of secret planes had a double mission in more than their official mission, that is to say monitor ET's comings and goings between Earth and space, and having himself observed 6 to 7 UFOs with other military personnel in Area 51.

Robert Salas, site incident witness Echo of Malmstrom;

Dwynne Arnesson (lieutenant-colonel, officer

USAF Electronic Communications)
declaring having received, while he was at the
base of Ramstein (Germany) a message relating
to a crash in Spitsbergen (Norway).

Harland Bentley (US Army first class)
claiming to have observed UFOs.

John Maynard (retired DIA) saying he saw
sensitive documents, including images
of UFOs.

Karl Wolf (USAF Sergeant) declaring to be
came to repair equipment at NASA
talked to someone who told him that there
had a base on the far side of the Moon.

Donna Hare (NASA employee), stating
having seen aerial photos of "circles"
flying over the Earth, and one of his
acquaintances would have told him that a vessel
had been seen during an Apollo mission.

Larry Warren (USAF Security Officer) on
the Bentwaters sighting.

George A. Filler, III (retired pilot of
aerial espionage at the USAF), statement having

observed UFO on mission, briefed from superiors on the observatin of Tehran, and having heard the account of the recovery of an alien killed by an MP.

Clifford Stone (Army Sergeant 1st Class US), claiming that the US government would have tried to destroy the evidence of the crash of a alien aircraft containing aliens land on Thursday, December 9, 1965 in Pennsylvania and allegedly threatened and penalized all likely to talk about this event, they would have witnessed:

"Some of them look so much like us, that they might be with us without us realizing it". He then clarified that 57 alien species had already been recorded.

Mark McCandlish (concept artist for the USAF), recounting that his father (USAF) had seen a UFO at the telescope, which a college friend had saw 3 UFOs and showing photographs of the saucer of Provo, and telling that a man Edwards base has also seen UFOs.

Daniel Sheehan (lawyer), testifying to the failed attempt by President Carter to retrieve secret UFO information.
He also testifies to having seen photos of crashed UFOs.

Carol Rosin (doctor, Aerodynamics Consultant) stating that Werner VonBraun would have made revelations about extraterrestrials within the framework of a space weapon that was needed to ban.

Greer finally concludes by demanding an end to the silence and especially the end of the plot, then responds to the questions from journalists.

The quote from German philosopher Arthur Schopenhauer seems to be well adapted to the context:

"All truth passes through three stages. First, it is ridiculed. Second, it is violently opposed. Third, it is accepted as being self-evident".

I.11. Contacted and abducted.

We can see that after the Hiroshima and
Nagasaki's nuclear bombs, the number of
UFO sightings and crashes are increasing. That
is also valid for the number of people
contacted and victims of abduction. even though
the two phenomena seem to be basically linked,
and they are in a way, but once the facts are
properly analyzed, we note that they diverge
considerably in form.
We have testimonials from contacted people
dating from before the "GREADA" treaty
(The "GREADA" treaty is the pact that
President Eisenhower signed in 1954 with the
"small grays"), on the other hand, all the
abduction testimonies begin after this agreement.

According to William Cooper, a soldier who worked from 1970 to 73 for Naval Intelligence Agency and who had access to top secret documents, the terms of this agreement are as follows:

1. The extraterrestrials (the little greys) undertake to not interfere in earthly affairs by in return, the terrestrial authorities undertake to not interfere in theirs.
2. The little grays, in exchange for new technologies, will have the right to abduct a number of humans and animals needed for their experiments. Humans, victims of this abduction, must be well treated and returned without any trauma. (No restrictions for animal abductions)
3. A list of abductees, including their number and names, must be submitted periodically to the United States government specifically at MJ12. (Majestic Twelve is the code name of a secret committee of scientists, military leaders, and government officials, formed in 1947 by an executive order of U.S. President Harry S. Truman. The group's main objective is to study extraterrestrial activity. MJ12 decides what should be leaked or hidden from the media...).

4. The extraterrestrials undertake not to sign
    agreements with other governments
    terrestrial than that of the United States.

Phil Schneider, a scientist who worked for the
United States government for projects of
construction of underground bases, also testify
the terms of this agreement. We can
cite other witnesses who were present during
the encounter with the little grays or other
senior people who read these reports
classified defense secret and having disclosed
these informations afterwards, like Michael Wolf
of the NSC or Major Philip Corso. According to
these last, a year after the agreement in 1955,
they realized that the contribution of technology
makes by the grays was minimal and that they
also had great doubt about the veracity of the
number and names of abductees whom they
claim were millions of times higher than
number that the grays communicated to them.
So theoretically, by definition, "abduction" is the
kidnapping of a person by extraterrestrial entities
which then delete everything memories of this
action. And these abductions all begin after 1954.
The victims of abduction tell us the facts during
regression hypnosis sessions and 99%
extraterrestrial entities described are the little
greys.

These victims are more and more numerous to manifest today.

One of the most incredible abduction stories is that of the Hill couple. It's the first and the best documented.

September 19, 1961,
in the car, on the way back from their holidays, the couple sees a white light in the sky. Barney Hill stops multiple times to check the position of the object and is persuaded that it follows them, he decides to stop the car one last time near Lancashire in New Hampshire, to observe the luminous craft using his binoculars, , and sees humanoids shapes observing them through the luminous windows of the craft; panicked, he goes back to his car and tries to flee the flying object, it takes a wooded side road, hoping that the trees will provide him with camouflage necessary for this but after a few turns, the couple is overtaken by the flying object which land in front of the car. They will be wrapped in a white light and their last memory will be the sound of several long beeps. After that, the couple find themselves in car, rolling 62 Miles from the place of their abduction, this is only after having seen the road sign "Concorde 17 Miles" that they understand that they traveled 35 Miles in a state of drowsiness, they finally arrive

home 2 hours late on their schedule. Once home, Betty and Barney find several anomalies. The watches they wore on their wrists had stopped function. There were claw marks on Barney's shoes and a pink powder that she couldn't explain, on Betty's dress.

The body of their car had circular traces on which Barney had the idea of place a compass, he found that the needles of it turned as if they were distraught. The following days Betty will make horrible nightmares, remembering the scenes of her experience.

Barney is not no better off.

The day after their abduction, Betty call the Pease military base to report this anomaly, she talks to Major Paul W. Henderson who confirms the presence of the UFO. The flying object had also been spotted by the military base radar.

More or less a month later, on Saturday 21 October, the couple receives Walter N. Webb, a NICAP Investigator, National Committee investigation of aerial phenomena, the investigator becomes aware of the facts, a evidence comes out the couple does not manage to relate what that they lived during these missing 2 hours in relation to their schedule, and during their journey of 35 Miles.

In the meantime the couple develops anxiety symptoms and mental disorders. They have oriented towards Doctor Benjamin Simon, the hypnotherapist will engage in weekly hypnosis and regression sessions with the couple. These sessions will last 7 months.

And the hypnosis sessions will reveal, their extraordinary story of abduction. The couple explains that he was captured by a dozen creatures they describe, 1m to 1m30 high, from large almond-shaped black eyes, a small mouth and two nostrils no nose, one head disproportionate to their lean bodies.

It is with the Hills that we discover for the first time the little greys.

The torque is brought inside the alien craft, placed in different chambers, and after a complete medical examination, they will be lying on an operating table.

Barney explains that, one of the entities, inserted him a sharp instrument in his genital organ trying to squeeze some fluid out of it.

Betty explains that one of the beings tried to introduce a pointed instrument at the level of his navel but seeing her suffer, he did not insist.

Next the entities showing Betty a map of their solar system, asked him to locate the planet Earth on a space map, Betty could not do it. Then the couple will be accompanied to their car, from where they observe the ship take off before getting back on the road.

For "persons contacted" the process and the beings encountered are completely different. The "persons contacted" are not as numerous as the people who are victims of abduction despite this their testimonials are of better quality, very detailed and above all spread over a longer period long. One of the first contacted in history is Georges Adamski. He will be contacted by a Venusian called Orthon. He will write several books dealing with the subject, these will have great success.
Will follow other contacted persons like Wayne Sulo Aho, Orfeo Angelucci, Bethurum Truman, Maurizio Cavallo, Daniel William Fry, Narciso Genovese, Sheila Gibson, Harry M. Gesner, Gabriel Green, Aarno Heinonen, Eric Julien, George King, Guy Kirkwood, Ken Macmillan, Laura Marxer, George Van Tassel, Howard Menger, Elizabeth Klarer, Alex Necklace and Billy Meier, to name only the best known.
It is people are contacted by extraterrestrials races like Lyrians, Venusians, alpha centaurians, andromedians and Pleiadians who are physically very close to humans. "Contacted Persons" maintain long-term relationships with these breeds and are very often invested of the

following objectives: raise the collective conscience to break free the Humanity from his shackles.

These alien races, across the contacted, work to make that humans realize their cosmic nature and exceptional ability.

Although the account of each contacted person present variations in the details, they seem nevertheless all follow the following pattern:

1. An internal impulse pushes the future "contacted" to be very interested in alien races aliens.

2. A first contact is established with the future contacted by telepathy. A sort of transfer of thought comforting him and preparing him for real touch.

3. Humans and aliens reunite in an uncrowded place.

4. The contacted person is invited to the alien vessel.

5. Contacted person agrees to continue meeting aliens or not.

6. If the contacted person agrees to continue, some
contacted testify to having traveled with the alien ship, Some around the Earth, while others testify to being taken to other planets.

7. A relationship of mutual trust is established. The contacted person, with the help of extraterrestrials, is responsible for awakening as much consciousness as possible.

The contacted person helps the alien race during their experiments they perform on Earth. We can see that the approach is more long, less aggressive and more respectful for the contacted human in relation to the abductions, which are often traumatic for the abducted person. Note, however, that abductions are not sessions of torture, the victims of abduction that relate their experience during the sessions of regression hypnoses and are not mistreated during the experiments carried out by the little greys.

Here is an example that perfectly illustrates these stages is the story of Elizabeth Klarer. Elizabeth Klarer is a South African born in 1910 in Mooi River, a remote region of Natal. From an early age Elizabeth amazes. Child,

145

she communicates and speaks the language of the tribes
neighbors of the family estate located at
Kwazala Natal in the Midlands, without having been there
initiated. She plays several instruments, has clairvoyance gifts and
telepathy. At the age of seven, while playing not far from the family estate with his sister
9-year-old Barbara, finds herself in front of
a silvered flying saucer. Some months later, Elizabeth plays outside of the
property and is in danger. A tornado approaches the little girl who will be saved by the intervention of this same silvered flying saucer.
But it was in 1954 that Elizabeth would really be contacted. The silvered saucer of his childhood is back, and shows himself to her on the hill of Cathkin. The ship remains hovering at
one meter from the floor for several minutes. Elizabeth Klarer describes the ship, as
silver colored, with a diameter of 18 meters, elliptical shape with a dome which
windows are visible, and through one of these windows, the young woman observed a humanoid being who was for her "the most beautiful being

146

of the universe". During the observation the saucer suddenly takes off vertically and disappears.

Months later the silver saucer returned to the same hill and this time Elizabeth Klarer felt it through his psychic abilities very developed and went to the hill of Cathkin like to honor a date planned.

Once there, she sees the silver saucer on the ground and next to it a humanoid being resembling perfectly the human but of extraordinary beauty. L' tall angelic being with gray hair clear and with a light golden complexion, presents himself and invites Elizabeth in the ship. His name is "Akon" and comes from a planet of Alpha Centauri.

Once in the ship, he will show his guest terrestrial, on a holographic screen, images of his planet and will present it to the other members of the crew. Akon will give information on the societal system of his planet, where police, army, politician, government and money do not exist. Each citizen exercises a self-monitoring, and acting ethically. Akon will also provide information on how to operation of his vessel which uses electromagnetic energy from the Earth. A free and infinite energy. Other topics will be

147

discussed like, how the alpha-centaurians managed to spread throughout the universe, their technologies, their philosophy based on the most great source of energy of the universe " The love".

After completing their mission, Akon and the members of his people returned to their planet. Elizabeth Klarer waited until to the end of her life for the return of the vessel, convinced that he was going to return take her with him to Alpha Centauri, but Akon did not return. Elizabeth Klarer died at the age of 84 and has left behind many testimonies of his contact, a ring
belonging to Akon, a stone from space and marvelous works. For example, the book "Beyond the light barrier".

I.12. The implants.

The implants are found on some abductees.
According to information gathered during the
regression sessions, they are all attributed to
"Zeta alien race", "the little grays". American
surgeon Roger K. Leir is one of the pioneers of
the phenomenon. The surgeon participated in 16
operations for implant extractions. These
implants after laboratory analysis, showed
non-terrestrial features. For Leir, the
implants are made of the same materials
than those of meteorites, and appear to be
manufactured objects, nanotechnology
alien emitting scalar waves, a different kind of
radiation electromagnetic. Nikola Tesla is the
first

who was able to demonstrate their existence. This are very penetrating waves in the form of spiral, having very different properties from electromagnetic waves discovered by Heinrich Hertz.

Apart from that, the fact that no trace of lesion and entry point into the body of the victims were observable, invalidates the skeptics hypothesis, who claim that implants are only ordinary objects, such as shards of glass or metal, which would have accidentally entered the bodies. According to ufologists, these implants have a function, to collect information about our emotions and reactions on behalf of the "little ones Grey".

The informations would serve, on the one hand, to cure the alien race of zeta-reticuli, who have become, following bad choices during their evolution as a species, beings devoid of emotions, the zeta-reticulis did the choice to remove all emotions from their beings, mistakenly thinking that these would harm the good development of their society, and in the others hand this information would be used to create a hybrid race. The representatives of this new "half-grey half-human" race will be destined to be the pioneers of a new race and a new world.

I.13. Press statements.

They come from the former astronauts of the
Apollo or Soyuz missions, aircraft pilots
And political leaders of some countries.
They deliver us their heartfelt testimonies. Apart
from, "risking of being ridiculous", these people
have nothing to gain by doing this, yet they share
their experiences and some information classified
as a defense secret at the risk of their career or
sometimes even their life. Those statements are
very precious:

**Dmitry Medvedev, former Russian prime
minister**, answers a question about
aliens thinking the cameras are off:

"In addition to the nuclear code case, the

president of the country receives a "top secret" file. Which is special. This file contains information about aliens that regularly visit our planet. Moreover, a report is submitted by a secret service, which in absolute secrecy, exercises control over the comings and goings of aliens on the territory. You can get more information on this subject, thanks to the well-known film directed by Barry Sonnenfeld "Men In Black". I would not tell the number of aliens that live among us, because this will cause panic".

Edgard Mitchell NASA Astronauts,
sixth to have walked on the Moon.
Reserve Astronaut for Apollo10, and astronauts of the Apollo 14 mission, will make several startling statements about the subject:

"We know UFOs are real. The question is: where do they come from?"

"When I was on the moon, 26 years ago, it was part of popular, religious and philosophical to believe that we were the center biology of the universe. Not long ago, there were still educated and cultured people that were for this theory".

"We all know UFOs are real.
From what I know today, from what
I have seen and experienced, I think the evidence
are formal and many of them are classified as top
secret by the government. »

Edgar Mitchell will also declare that
military devices used the technology
of a captured and dismantled alien ship.

**Scott Carpenter, astronaut and second
American to orbit the Earth:**

"At no time while they were in space, the
astronauts were alone, they were
permanently watched by UFOs"

**John Herschel Glenn, astronaut, pilot of
hunter and American politician.** Glenn is
the first American to perform an orbital flight
around the Earth:

"In those glorious days, I was very
uncomfortable
when we were asked to say things
that we didn't want and to deny it hast
others, and yet we have seen things
there, strange things. And we couldn't say
anything. »

Cosmonaut Georgy M. Grechco:

"If I were free to say what I saw in space, the world would be amazed."

Dick D'Amato, National Security Specialist and member of the National Security Council United States declared in 1991:

"An occult faction of the government kept secret the UFO information"

Former Minister of Defense of Canada Paul Hellyer in 2005, said at a conference release at the University of Toronto:

"UFOs are as real as airplanes that fly above our heads."

Gordon Cooper, American astronaut Mercury program, manned orbitals flight program, declare in a speech that he will do in the stands of the U.N. in 1985:

"I believe that these spaceships and their crews who visit Earth from other planets are obviously a bit more technologically advanced than us. I think that we need a program

coordinated at a very high level to collect and
scientifically analyze the data of
the whole planet on the different types
meetings to determine how
best interact with our visitors from a
friendly manner. First we should
show them that we have learned to solve
our problems in a peaceful way, rather
than war, before being accepted as full member
of the universal team.
This admission would provide our world with
fantastic opportunities for progress in all
areas. It would therefore seem certain that the
United Nations have a vested right to treat
this subject appropriately and promptly. During
For years I've lived with a secret, the secret
imposed on all specialists and astronauts. I
can now reveal that every day, at
United States our radars detect objects of
shape and nature unknown. There are thousands
of witness reports and quantities of reports
who prove it, but no one wants to give them
back
public. Why ? Because the authorities have
fear that people will imagine a species
horrible invaders. So the key word
remains: We must avoid panic at all
price. »

Another day, during an interview, he says:

"As far as I am concerned, there are far too many examples of unexplained UFO sightings in the world to eliminate the possibility of a extraterrestrial life."

Another astronaut from the Mercury program Donald Slayton says:

I was doing a test flight on a P-51 fighter at Mineapolis, when I spotted this object. It was about 10,000 feet, it was a fine afternoon sunny. As I got closer, this looked like a sounding balloon, gray and of a diameter of about 1 meter. But as soon as I put myself behind this thing, it did not look like a weather balloon anymore. It looked like a disk saucer. The same instant, I realized that he was moving away from me and I was there flying over 500km/h; I continued for a few moments and then suddenly this thing has simply took off. She climbed with an angle of 45° in turning and accelerating and was simply gone. Two days later, I took a beer with my commander and I thought to myself "Damn, I should talk to him about it".vI did, and he told me to go to information and report to them.

I did, and I never heard of it again.

Robert Oppenheimer and Albert Einstein in the conclusions of their report commissioned by the NSA said:

"We not only declare that the entities extraterrestrials exist but they also visited Earth for thousands of years".

The astronaut who participated in the Apollo 9 project and Gemini IV, James McDivitt said:

In 1965, during the Gemini IV mission. I was looking out the porthole when I saw a cylindrical object to which was attached a pipe or an antenna. A photo came out after that did not correspond at all to the object I had seen. It looked more like spots of light.

Leaked radio conversation from 1969, between the base in Houston and astronaut Pete Conrad during the Apollo 12 mission:

P.Conrad: - There is an object behind us, it turns on itself. He's still the same distance, it looks like he's following us.

Houston: - Roger, Pete the item you have

spotted near the porthole, we think he could be one of the panels.

P.Conrad: - It could be true but when we turned around, I saw one of these objects jump at a very high speed.
153

Yevgeni Khrunov, cosmonaut and pilot of Soyuz 5 states:

"As far as UFOs are concerned, their presence cannot be denied. Thousands of people have seen it."

Dr. Brian O'Leary, Astronaut Candidate and scientist. Author of the book "Why I refused to go to the moon. »

"There is abundant evidence that we have been contacted, that civilizations have visited us during a very long time. that their appearance is weird, from any kind of point of view traditional Western materialism. That these visitors use technologies of the consciousness, they use toroids, they use co-rotating discs for their system of propulsion, which seems to be the denominator common of the UFO phenomenon."

**Mr. Gabriel Voisin, pilot, builder
aeronautics and aviation pioneer:**

"These extraterrestrial explorers are separated
from us by a barrier more impassable than
the Himalayas: our technical backwardness and
our high ignorance."

I.14. Alien races that have visited Earth.

In an interview, Clifford Stone a veteran of the US military informs us that there are more than 50 known and listed extraterrestrial races in a catalog of 1000 pages, which according to him would be a first aid manual in case of contact with these different races. There are sources that give us the same number of races like the Russian alien book of KGB.

Here, we have taken up the 11 most observed alien races. According to the information that we have been able to obtain from the bodies recovered after UFOs crashs, testimonies of soldiers, the classified reports, testimonies during the regression sessions.

The extraterrestrial races are classified according to 6 criteria, their galactic origin, their morphology, behavior (their degree of threat), their frequency of appearances, their special abilities and in "details".

1. The Zeta Reticulans.

Origin:

They originate from a Binary Star located at a distance of 39 light-years from the Earth in the southern reticulum constellation.

Morphology:

Small gray 90 to 130cm. Humanoid bodies, trunk of body and limbs very thin. They only have 4 fingers in their hands. Their heads are big and disproportionate to their bodies, with large almond-shaped black eyes.

Frequency:

Very frequent appearances, the small grays are the most observed aliens on Earth.

Behavior:

Neutral and sometimes aggressive, Zetas collaborate with humans but this collaboration can be dangerous in the long run given that the race is under the control of the terrestrial military-industrial complex and of the draconian race.

Details:

The Zetas are one of two alien races we have a pact with. Very intelligent Race but without feelings.

Since 1954. They are authorized to make experiments on humans. The large majority people who were victims of abduction, describe the grays during their regression sessions.

With these experiments, the grays try to regain some of the skills they lost, according to some ufologists during a nuclear war, according to others, the grays are cyborgs serving their Reptilians or Draconians masters; anyway, the gray are victims of genetic stagnation and searches for a cure via our DNA.

Specialty:

They have great knowledge in genetics, they are known to be the geneticists of the universe.

2. The Tall Whites.

Origin:

They originate from the Constellation of Orion, from the red supergiant star Betelgeuse. Distance from Earth 642.5 light-years.

Morphology:

The Tall whites are of the humanoid type, they are with a length of approximately 2,5 meters. Their skin is very clear or even dull.

Frequency:

Their presence is limited to Indiana Springs, in a military base where they have been assigned a special area. The tall whites are our galactic refugees.

Behavior:

Neutral

Details:

The tall whites made contact with the United States government in 1954; and have asked for "a right of asylum"; claiming their planet would have become uninhabitable because of the future extinction of their sun. They work in collaboration with the US military, and help to improve their technology.

Specialty:

Genetics and mind control.

3. The Draconian.

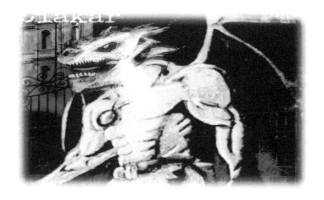

Origin:

They originate from the Constellation of the
Dragon, from the star "Alpha Draconis".
Distance from Earth 303.3 light years.

Morphology:

Reptilians 4 to 6 meters high and 800 kg.
They look like giant lizards, their bodies
are covered with scales of green, brown and
sometimes reddish.

Frequency:

Rare, we talk about them in many religious and mythological writings.

Behavior:

Aggressive and dangerous.

Details:

The draconian race is the oldest of the universe. A race of colonizers and soldiers, they have many colonies in the Milky Way. Having visited Earth in time elders, some assume they are the masters earth reptilians and grays that they manipulate.

Specialty:

Highly developed physical and mental aptitude. Military and colonizer.

4. Les lyriens.

Origin:

They originate from the Constellation of Lyra, 26.5 light years from Earth.

Morphology:

A large majority are of humanoid types, they look exactly like humans. But different types of hybrid lyrian are also known, such as feline humanoids, birds, reptilian and insectoids.

Frequency:

Impossible to determine because the Lyrian humanoids can blend perfectly in our society and the hybrids of this race are mentioned in rare testimonials. In some holy writings, rock paintings or in the stories of Egypt.

Behavior:

Friendly

Details:

The Lyrians are considered our distant ancestors. They are at the origin of our presence on Earth. The Lyrians are one of the oldest races of the galaxy, the race possesses many colonies in the Milky Way. The belief is that we would be seeded by this alien race on our planet. The vegans, procyonians, pleiadians and us humans derive from the Lyrians.

Specialty:

Historian, galactic archivist. Geneticist and explorer. If we should look for our origins, we know where to turn.

5. The Vegans.

Origin:

They originate from The Constellation of Lyra, from the Star Vega.
Distance from Earth 26.5 light years

Morphology:

They are of humanoid types, they descended from the Lyrians. The color of their skin is bluish.

Frequency:

Rare

171

Behavior:

Friendly

Details:

Vegans seem to be basically the same race than the Lyrians. They would have left their home planet following a civil war.
Both vegans and lyrians have visited the Earth in remote times of our History,
at the beginning of the first civilizations. In the Hindu scriptures one of the three deities "Vishnu" is always represented from blue skin Like vegans. The race also seems to compete in space exploration and colony formation, with the lyrians.

Specialty:

Explorer

6. The Procyonians.

Origin:

They originate from the Constellation of the little dog, from the binary star system of Procyon, from one of the 6 planets in the procyonian solar system. The planets of this solar system are relatively small compared to the earth. distance from Earth, 11.4 light years.

Morphology:

2 different types are observed, the first is humanoid, and perfectly resemble the humans with some small

173

differences their complexion can be white, greenish or Brown. Their eyes are bigger and their smaller ears. They occupy the 4th planet of procyonian system.

The second type is amphibo-reptoid these have the appearance of a large scaly lizard from 2.10m to 2.50m with yellow and red brown eyes. They occupy the 2nd and 3rd planet of the Procyonian system.

Frequency:

Rare

Behavior:

Neutral, friendly

Details:

Both breeds seem to have migrated to the solar system of Procyon to flee a disaster. Humanoids migrated from Sirius b while the reptoid-amphibians of the cancer constellation.

Specialty:

Explorer

7. The Pleiadians.

Origin:

They originate from the Constellation of Taurus, from the star cluster of Pleiades. Distance from Earth 444 years-light

Morphology:

Similar to Norse-looking humans at few differences. The Pleiadians are in average longer and have a life expectancy much longer than humans.

Frequency:

Frequent; almost all contacted persons describe beings similar to the Pleiadians.

Behavior:

Friendly

Details:

The Pleiadians are the descendants of the
Lyrians.
The human contactees all describe beings
angelic and friendly. The Pleiadians are also
the first extraterrestrial race that warned the
General Eisenhower in 1954 facing the threat
grays. They define their mission on Earth
as follows: To help humanity free itself from
all oppressive structures and accompany it
so that it acquires a high level of
awareness.

Specialty:

Explorer and Geneticist.

8. The Andromedans.

Origin:

They originate from the Constellation of
Andromeda. Distance from Earth
350 light years away. Not to be confused with
the Galaxy of Andromeda.

Morphology:

They are humanoids with light blue complexion.
Their eyes are a bit bigger. Their bluish color
turns towards white as they age. An
Andromedan can live 2000 terrestrial years.

Frequency:

Quite frequent, many contacted us give details of their species, the latest in date is Alex Collier.

Behavior:

Neutral, friendly.

Details:

Andromedans are a very ancient race peaceful, of scientists. Through Alex Collier one of the contacted by the breed, they learn us a lot about ourselves. our past and probable future. According to the Andromedans, our race like all other races humans originate from the constellation of the lyre. Our race would have come from another galaxy in a still non-human, settled form in the constellation of the lyre more precisely in a planet of the Vega system, where our evolution in human form began. We can mention the genius hypothesis genetics of our hosts which would be the basis of our transformation. What is also strange is that they compare our universe to a hologram which would be 21 billion years old. That joins the work of several scientists

terrestrial presenting this as for example
the holographic universe of Michael Talbot.
They are part of a federation of 140 systems.
According to them the earth is under the
influence draconian and it will be entirely
directed by these tyrants in 2352.
Andromedans give us information about the
underground bases of the grays on Phobos, Mars
and our moon where humans would also be
present. Of the reptilian presence on our planet
some blending into the mass of others living
underground. They give us finally some details
on our moon, this one would be an artificial star.

Specialty:

Scientist.

9. The Sirians

Origin:

They originate from the Constellation of Canis
Major, from Sirius solar system,
distance from Earth, 8.3 light years. Sirius is
the brightest star in the earth's sky.

Morphology:

There are several different species that coexist in
the Sirius system, both physical and non-
physical, humanoids and non-humanoids. The
majority of sirians resemble humans. They are
red, beige, gray, black and bluish. They are
slightly longer than humans and their heads are

180

bigger, this is because they have an extra lobe at the level of the forehead due to the size of their brains just like whales and dolphins.

There are also the aquatic beings "the nommos", reptilians, and a type of humanoid bipeds feline called "the katayys"

Frequency:

Rare, their visits seem spaced thousands sometimes tens of thousands of years but they are regular.

Behavior:

85% friendly except those of reptilian types who are hostile to us.

Details:

The Sirians have been visiting Earth for millions of years. They are the origin of Homo sapiens. One theory is that with the help of lyrians, arcturians and pleiadians, the sirians delivered to experiments on a race of backward humanoids living on Earth and have modified the DNA of this one, by adding theirs. Which gave Homo sapiens. The sirians havebeen in contact with humans since

181

Lemuria. Egyptians, Mayans and closer from us canned dogon african tribe still has traces.

Specialty:

Explorer, geneticist, healer, scientist.

10. The Alpha Centaurians.

The dark knight, centaurian aircraft.

Origin:

They originate from Alpha centaur planetary system. It's the closest planetary system to the ours with the central star Proxima Centauri. Distance from Earth 4.24 light years.

Morphology:

Alpha Centaurians are identical to humans.

Frequency:

Due to their almost identical morphology to humans, it is impossible to know exactly the frequency of their visit.

Behavior:

Friendly

Details:

The Alpha centaurians are ahead of the humans but the technology gap is not large compared to other alien races. According to the testimonies of former Americans soldiers, a protocol would exist to contact them. Alpha Centaurians are a race that rejects all competitions and competition between beings, they find it harmful and advocate freedom individual and social justice. They want to help humans to raise them to a higher level of consciousness.

Specialty:

Explorer

11. The Arcturians.

Origin:

They originate from Herdsman constellation, from Arcturus solar system, distance from Earth 36.66 light years.

Morphology:

Arcturians are difficult to describe, they are multidimensional beings, they can take very varied physical forms; despite this, general form of humanoid type of 1,5 meters long, blue in complexion, and possessing a large brain seems to stand out.

Frequency:

Rare

Behavior:

Friendly

Details:

The Arcturians are one of the oldest races of the universe. They are technologically very advanced, the most advanced in the known universe according to them. Like the alpha centaurians helping our race so that it reaches a higher level of awareness, acturians seem to be responsible for a similar mission but at the scale of the universe. It is also one of the 4 races present during the DNA experiments carried out on our ancestors and creating Homo sapiens.

Specialty:

No need to list them, they are at the forefront of everything that is done in terms of technology. This race has reached a very high level of consciousness, and uses knowledge to help and to heal spiritually the less evolved races.

186

Chapter II: Dialectical.

"We declare that the extraterrestrial entities exist and visit Earth for thousands of years".

Robert Oppenheimer and Albert Einstein.

II.1. The ancient astronaut theory.

The ancient astronaut theory is a
theory which attempts to prove that the ancient
civilizations would have been in contact with the
aliens. This proximity would have allowed them
to acquire new technologies in various areas.
This theory is mentioned by many authors like
Louis Pauwels and Jaques Bergiers in
1960, Eva Blavatsky in 1870, Robert Charroux
in 1962, Jean Sendy in 1965 and by Erich Von
Daniken in 1968.
The theory is denigrated by the majority of the
scientific community, despite the fact that it
would solve, if approved, the problems of our
official historical chronology.
My goal in this part is not to
prove the veracity of all the points of this
theory, but only to try to understand

189

if extraterrestrial entities could have visit us. Apart from the representations of men in spacesuit and flying objects in the shape of discs in the cave paintings, the example below proves, by itself, that a contact has indeed took place:

At the end of the 19th and beginning of the 20th century, the Aborigines of Melanesia in Oceania see land for the first time on their islands, American and Japanese modern men.

These modern men arrive with a plane, boat made of metal and with all kinds of products manufactured, that they are delivered by air or sea freighter.

The Aborigines are of course amazed by this ballet of technology, magic in their eyes; and can non imagine, the factories and the incredible economic machine hiding behind it. After the departure of these modern men, the Melanesians have developed all sorts of rituals and beliefs which consists in imitating these in hoping to achieve the same effect. The aborigines have built tracks of landings, model planes, fictitious wooden operating cabins and control towers.

This is how "the cargo cult" was born.

It was born like this "the cargo cult".

This example illustrates the reaction that can result from contact between two civilizations with a huge technological gap.

So why, the representations of discal objects and men in spacesuits in the cave paintings, would not prove that our ancestors would have taken the extraterrestrial humanoids for gods. why it wouldn't have had the same effect on our ancestors. This is perfectly possible.

II.2. Eisenhower and the contract.

Dwight Eisenhower is the 34th President of the United States. He served two terms from 1953 to1961. Of military training, he was also the Supreme Commander to the "Allied forces" during World War II. the President Eisenhower is also known to have make a secret deal with an alien race. That race would be a variant of the "Grey".

Facts:

February 1954, when he had just returned from Georgia, where he had just spent his winter holidays, President Eisenhower hastily leaves for Palm Springs in California, from 17 to 24 February, to carry out, a second time, his winter holidays. No communication will be made to the press with regard to its holiday program. In Palm Springs, the 20 February, the President disappears. The press is alarmed, some even suppose that that the President would be dead. The spokesperson for the President announces to calm speculators that this disappearance is due to a problem of tooth, which occurred during a dinner, and that the president

needed urgent medical attention. the health issue is actually a pretext to hide the truth. because on the night of February 20, President Eisenhower and a select committee of advisors are on the Muroc military base, later renamed Edwards AFB, for a historic encounter with an alien race. According to sources close to the president, the plane of the president landed on the tarmac, and instead of heading towards the base terminal, the plane went park at the end of the runway. The entries and outings to the military base are prohibited, and the staff, except those authorized, see each other restrict their movement.

The radars of the base are cut off, and after a while six alien spaceships fly over the base. Two of them cigar-shaped and four disc-shaped. One of the saucers lands near the plane of the President while the other five remain in flight stationary above these. Two humanoid type entities come out of the saucer, the president goes to meet them with his bodyguards and advisers, and talks with one of the two humanoids.

The testimonials:

This historic meeting is attested by many testimonials. One of them comes from the author known for his work in metapsychic Gerald Light. By a series of letter, sent in April 1954, the author explains his great meeting. He even writes in one of the letters that President Eisenhower had intended to reveal to the whole world but he was dissuaded by the senior ranks of the army.

We can also mention as a witness, the Economic Advisor to President Edwin Nourse, the representative of the Vatican Cardinal James Francis Mcintyre and Franklin Winthrop Allen, a member of the "Hearst" press group.
This meeting is also attested by indirect sources, for example William Cooper, who worked between 1970 and 73, for the service of naval intelligence. Cooper had access to the document classified as a defense secret.

After having describes the aircraft and the morphology of extraterrestrials, he continues: the first humanoid extraterrestrials race, warned the President Eisenhower of the presence in Earth orbit of a dangerous alien race and they asked them not to deal under any pretext with this second alien race. The first alien race offered to help the human race to reach a high level in spiritualism and in return demanded to annihilate all terrestrial nuclear arsenal; They also added that no sharing of technology was possible as long as humans continue killing each other, polluting and destroying the Earth by using its resources irresponsibly.

There was no agreement with this breed. We also have the son of Commander Charles Sugg's who almost has the same name as Charles L. Suggest's. In an interview he gave After being retired from the Marines, Charles L.

Suug's said:

My father was present on February 20, 1954 with President Eisenhower and he said he saw two Nordic-like extraterrestrial entities with long white hair and dull blue eyes and a very fair complexion, the first humanoid was at a few steps from the President, he was not allowed to approach closer and the second stood further back at the level of their flying saucer.

The entity claimed to come from another solar system and wanted details of our trials of nuclear bomb. Or the son of William Lear, who is the founder of the Lear jet company, William Lear was also the close friend of the director of the CIA, William Colby. According to Lear, a first extraterrestrial race had warned the President about a second race.

President Eisenhower's great-granddaughter, Laura Eisenhower adds fuel to the flame with her disclosures, here is an excerpt from his interview with Alfred Lambremont Webre, as part of his show named "the alien invasion has already taken place":

A.Lambremont: - In a extremely shocking statement, you say: "there is a massive cover-up regarding extraterrestrial contact with our governments, and a great secrecy with regard to those who have been victims of abduction or have been contacted."

And the key is in what you say: "It's because he already had an invasion and they don't want us to know."

Laura Eisenhower: - There are a lot of things. We face reptilians, who ended up living illegally. They were not necessarily malevolent, but those who come from the Draco star system are part of a plan for the enslavement of humanity. So we are dealing with many different species, and the invasion lies in the manipulation, mind control. That would be the manipulation of our mind by controlling the dark technologies, the same technologies who want to control nature, who want to control humans; ; with the "chemical trails" "HAARP technology", What we can see or read in the mass media , what we see coming from religion and government; you see this manipulation mass? where most people don't even recognize what is happening because it seems to be a part of the human experience, and by seeing the level of manipulation and control, I would say that the invasion has already taken place and worked for thousands and thousands of years and when we deal with something like the illuminati or illuminati or some institutions of these shadow government, there are a lot of factions and they do this kind of infighting, but they all fight for the control of the human race, it is not really our sovereignty, the truth, they forbid us to see reality. It's like we're some kind of byproduct of complex power games between multiple factions.

When we speak of a contract, we think about Eisenhower's contract only but in fact Roosevelt and Hitler had also had contacts with these extraterrestrial entities and had contracts. They both encountered the first humanoid race and both were rejected their plan in favor of the grays and their technology. The Nazis seem to have acquired the technology of control mental and for the Americans, it was more technologies that revolve around metal and free energy, things that could just improve their daily life but after operation "paperclip" the United States has recovered mind control technology to the Nazi scientists.
I think originally some of these technologies should help us, against the potential threats as a form of defense, but these industries of defense have been infiltrated.
I also think that the Zionists and the nazis are in this ghost government, and they're on the same team.
It's as though there was some kind of chess game between them and that we would be excluded.
It was not about signing a treaty, it was rather about surrending and that the Western countries

were not necessarily refused, it was that they just weren't able to come to an agreement with each other, because there were so many different points of view and because the umbrella corporation and MJ12 had already been established.

The rivalry between these different factions did not allow for a concise decision on the matter; And in this climate of uncertainty, so when we were most vulnerable, the Greys came up with their technology, and we had no choice but to accept it.

Everything was planned this way since a long time ; it's not some kind of spontaneous thing, like "oh whoops" what have we done! We have making a deal with the devil! We sold ourselves to grey! Everything was strategically planned and that's also linked with the "Rockefellers" and the "Bilderbergs" you know, everything had been done beforehand for this to happen and then to say: it was Ike's or another person's fault. (Ike is Dwight Eisenhower's nickname).

II.3 Evidences on Mars and the Moon.

NASA said in April 2015 that within 20 years
we will have proof of extraterrestrial life
in our galaxy. At first sight it was very
exciting that such a statement finally comes
from an official space administration like NASA.
But once the subject had been thoroughly
studied, we realize that Nasa is talking about
microbial-like life. This article must have made
many ufologists and astronomer smile.
NASA still operates the same way.
To begin with they deny the information and try
to discredit it, then no longer denies it, to
approve it and finally before the pressure of
multitude evidences from ufologists
and astronomers, we see appearing this kind
of statement, lacking in boldness. This way

to proceed causes to waste precious time to Humanity.

The same operational pattern is observed for NASA statements about signs "life on Mars". When the first ufologists declared, almost 20 years ago, that there was water on Mars and that NASA was hiding the truth from us, they were laughed at. But we have seen that they were right. NASA has first said there was water but only in the poles and in solid form, then in liquid form but seasonal. The analysis of photos and videos of the "rover Opportunity", active from 2004 to 2018 on the surface of the red planet, allows us to affirm that it is not only liquid water but also moving liquid on Mars like streams, and even vegetation.

The author of science-fiction and at the same time scientific, Arthur C. Clarke after analyzing the pictures of "Opportunity" said "there is vegetation on Mars, and NASA must declare it!"

We also observe these strange UFOs present frequently on the videos and photos sent by the "opportunity" and "curiosity" rovers; on which no official communication is made, as if these phenomena did not exist and were the work of a collective paranoia.

201

The giant monolith found on Phobos,
one of the moons of Mars, is an anomaly that
no one can explain yet. Top of 120 meters with
these forms at right angles. The monolith
appears to be a man-made structure.
According to Arthur C. Clarke, it is a gift from
the aliens. Buzz Aldrin, the second man
to have walked on the moon, as well as amateur
astronomer Efrain Palermo attract
attention to the phenomenon, which for them is
not natural. Unfortunately, we don't know more
of the Phobos monolith.

Ufologists are convinced that life existed on the
surface of the planet Mars. Presently a life on its
surface, which is inhospitable, seems impossible
but a life in its depths is more than likely. That
information will one day be disclosed by the
officials, I hope they don't take 50 years to do it
just like the presence of water on the planet.

The moon.

Our moon is a unique phenomenon in
the universe, a miracle in itself, by its
formation, positioning, size and influence on our
planet.
It slows down the speed of rotation of the Earth,
and allows it to maintain its inclination

23.5 degrees which is at the origin of the seasons, without the stabilizing effect of the Moon, our Earth would waver and it would beget irregular seasons.

If the Moon disappeared, the Sun would become the only star to influence the tides, then high tides would occur every day at noon and midnight, it will also influence the ocean currents and weather.

If the Moon did not exist, the Earth would be very different, it would be aligned with the axis of the equator by relation to the sun which would generate temperature differences ranging from minus 80 to over 100 degrees Celsius. While part of the Earth would be frozen another part would burn. Without the Moon the terrestrial flora and fauna would be very different and less varied.

But apart from its benefits on our planet, **what do we really know about the Moon?**

In fact, we have little knowledge about our Moon. Even today, all the theories on the formation of our satellite, remain hypotheses. Whether it is the theory of co-accretion, fission, capture, giant impact or of multiple impacts all present shortcomings. In other words, we still don't know how our moon was formed.

A second point that these theories fail to
demonstrate is the axis of rotation of the Moon
relation to the Earth, which is not at the level of
the, which is not at the level of the
Earth's equator, as with most
satellites in relation to their planets, but rather
inclined on average by 5% compared to that
of the ecliptic.
The third anomaly is the size of
our satellite. Our moon is one of the largest in
our solar system, only Titan, Ganymede, Io and
Calisto exceed the size of our moon; but these
moons, belonging to Saturn and Jupiter, are tiny
compared to the size of their planet, while our
moon is more than 1/4 the size of the Earth.
The synchronous rotation of the moon relative
to the Earth is also a strange phenomenon that
makes the Moon always presents to us its same
face.
The distance between the Earth and the Moon
and the dimensions of the Moon which allow
relative to its distance from the Sun, to obscure
perfectly the Sun, is also a strange and unique
phenomenon.
The moon seems to be hollow and resonates like
a bell after an impact.
At the end of the Apollo 12 mission, the lunar
module is intentionally spat on the surface of our

satellite. The Moon would have reasoned for a hour, proof that it could be hollow.

Other similar experiences caused the same result as the detonations of bombs placed by astronauts on its surface or the crash of the S-IVB rocket of the Apollo 16 mission.

Some craters also present anomalies. After the impact of an asteroid, the crater formed by it must be concaved in shape. While the ones on the Moon are convex.

After analyzing its nucleus, scientists deduce that the Moon would be almost a billion years older than the Earth. Moreover, the mineral composition of lunar rocks, brought on Earth following the many Apollo missions, vary considerably from the ones we find on Earth. Let us cite as an example the abundance of titanium on the Moon or even the presence of other transformed metals such as mica and brass. We also find on that the Moon radioactive elements such as uranium 236 and neptunium which that is not found naturally on Earth. Another troubling aspect of moon rocks were the fact that they were all magnetized.

We can add the anomalies all UFO sightings made by amateur astronomers, in which we clearly see shapes luminous rays taking off from the surface of the Moon or UFOs squadrons going towards it.

And finally, the photos taken by the
NASA astronauts during missions
Apollo and those of the many probes, prove
the presence of artificial structure on the surface
of our satellite. In these leaked photos
after 45 years, we observe forms
resembling antennas, military bases,
traces of displacement, strange lights
emanating from craters and other structures
artificial. Since these structures are not the work
of man, we can easily deduce that the Moon is
occupied by one or more extraterrestrial races.

II.4. The fake alien invasion.

The military-industrial complex will do anything to hide the truth about extraterrestrials from us. We saw it with the projects "Sign", "Blue books" and currently "Aquarius". The goal of this shadow government is keeping us down in a state of drowsiness so that humans don't raise awareness of their true cosmic nature and amazing abilities. But what is being planned is more complex and vicious. The military-industrial complex holds the extraterrestrial technology for a very long time. They do not deny the extraterrestrials. In the domain of ufology, a void such a feeling of doubt is voluntarily maintained in relation to aliens. Why? Because this "doubt" has enormous advantages for the shadow government.

Nowadays, the military in the services of government have the technology to imitate the shape and functioning of UFOs. In case false flag invasion, they will use "Made in USA" UFOs in the shape of a boomerang, saucer, cigar, pyramidal shape and triangular.

If we were to compare this to a card game, the extraterrestrials would be in the hands of the military-industrial complex, a joker.

Surely you have all noticed the cycle of terror to which is subject the Humanity i.e. economic-crises, virus, war and terrorist attacks, some will add to this list "pseudo-natural disasters". The names of economic crises, viruses, enemies and terrorist groups change but the cycle remains unchanged. The climate of terror must be maintained.

Here is a timeline showing the main lines of this cycle. Communicable Diseases and local Conflicts are not mentioned, let's focus on crises that have affected the whole world directly or indirectly:

1873-1896: Economic crisis "the long depression".

1914-1918: 1st World War.

1918-1919: Spanish flu 50 to 100 million deaths..

1929 – 1930: Economic crisis "the great depression" stock market crash.

1940-1945: World War II.

1947-1991: Cold War, arms race, context with a multitude of tensions in which, the World lives many facts at high tension but the two superpowers USA and USSR do not openly war each other.

1956 – 1958: Asian flu 4 million deaths.

1961 to 1989: Nationalist terrorist movements like ETA, IRA, ASALA... and a multitude of far-left terrorist movements.

1987: Creations of Al-Qaeda use against the USSR.

1989: Fall of the Berlin Wall.

1991: End of the cold war. End of the USSR.

1992: Al-Qaeda and Islam replace the hereditary enemy, the USSR no longer being, the military industrial complex needs a new enemy common.

2007-2012: Economic crisis, "crisis of subprime". The great recession.

2009 – 2010: H1N1 flu 150 to 575 thousand dead.

2006: Creations of DAECH.

2019: Covid19 pandemic, more than 6.800.000 deaths.

2020: Specialists announce a new economic crisis after covid19.

You can see that the world did not have a lot of respite. Citizens of Earth are like puppets trying to stay alive and to deal with trials imposed by an invisible hand. The latest virus created and spread by the man on the planet demonstrates it in a very significant way. At this stage you are entitled to ask yourself the following question, what is the relationship of the cycle of terror with a false alien attack?

The common enemy of the West was the USSR and the communism, after the fall of the Berlin wall, the communism ceases to be a threat and is gradually replaced by the supposed Islamist terrorism, first Al Qaeda, which is its

progressively replaced by DAECH, and once the terrorist threat averted, the new enemy common will be of extraterrestrial origin,
many ufologists warn us against to a false flag military operation. The tactic is known, it consists in attacking oneself even to then accuse the enemy, this allows to rally public opinion to his cause. To begin, they will declare they will declare that the extraterrestrials exist but unfortunately for us that they are hostile to us. We have a multitude of films dealing with the subject "Independence Day", "War of the Worlds" ... the Earth is attacked by aliens and then rescued by the United States military. This scenario is embedded in the collective subconscious and the day of the false Extraterrestrial attack will take place, the average person will have no trouble accepting it, the protests and warnings of the few refractory person won't change anything. The alien attack will be the ultimate threat that will unify the whole planet under one government, that of the new world order.

According to Carol Rosin, manager of "Fairchild Industries" Wernher Von Braun on his death bed, the warning against this scenario:

"After the USSR, the terrorist threat and some third world countries, the last map will be that of the extraterrestrials and it will be a lie".

If you have any doubts about this worthy scenario from a science fiction film, allow me to make you notice that the process is real, and even seems to have accelerated.

April 2020, the Pentagon shared several videos in which UFOs appear hunted down by airplane pilots. The Pentagon has not only shared these videos but also formalized the UFO phenomenon, it is a first in history, an official space administration declares UFOs are real. This statement will be the first of a long series. The statement will follow its existence, this time not just UFOs, but many aliens. Then will finally come to the statement "yes the extraterrestrials exist, but unfortunately they are hostile". You know the rest, but it's not all, fake alien attack is only the last link in the chain.

According to the famous magazine "the Economist", we observe in a caricature, the Earth and the Covid19 virus represented by two boxers on one ring clashing. The Earth seems to win the first round against the virus but behind the virus outside the ring waits, another opponent twice as tall and robust as the covid19, called "climate change". The earth will face it for its second round major natural (or pseudo-natural) disasters.

212

Before that just after defeating covid19, a big wave of vaccination will begin and in the process the chip implants (announced for 2025-2030 by the Founder and executive chairman of World Economic Forum Klaus Schwab).
You have the right to have doubts about the microchip implantations on humans, I invite you to consult this license deposited by Microsoft, on 20-06-2019, under the name of:

"WO2020060606", "CRYPTOCURRENCY SYSTEM USING BODY ACTIVITY DATA".

Here is its description:

Human body activity associated with a task provided to a user may be used in a mining process of a cryptocurrency system. A server may provide a task to a device of a user which is communicatively coupled to the server. A sensor communicatively coupled to or comprised in the device of the user may sense body activity of the user. Body activity data may be generated based on the sensed body activity of the user. The cryptocurrency system communicatively coupled to the device of the user may verify if the body activity data satisfies one or more conditions set by the cryptocurrency system, and award cryptocurrency to the user whose body activity data is verified.

"A sensor coupled in such a way as to communicate with a device the user, or included in it can detect the bodily activity of the user."

The project thus presented at first seems sight beneficial to humanity. It's similar to a person playing mini games, or would complete mini tasks to earn cryptocurrency with his smartphone, except that here the smartphone is the Human and the tasks will not be mini games on the net but tasks in real life.

Many of us will try to reassure themselves by telling themselves that, there is nothing wrong with to earn money in an easy way. But make no mistake, once this project is applicable on a global scale, I strongly doubt that the tasks to be performed will be as simple as going to buy a loaf of bread in a bakery. The possibilities are endless, and knowing the Human and his capacity to trample the moral, to harm the community for money, I dare not imagine the consequences disasters of this project.

If extraterrestrial civilizations with thousands of years ahead of our military technology were really hostile, and decided to attack us, the armies of the World united would be destroyed in a nanosecond. The extraterrestrial races are therefore not hostile, they don't reason like us, they are detached from all kinds of egos and desires imperialists who are our characteristics. Unfortunately, we are a race backward and aggressive ruled by our 2%, the wealthier, who seem to have a large problem with humanity. I fear that these sociopaths do not hesitate to annihilate the planet and to decimate its population, which they consider too numerous and unnecessary, for more money, power or just to satisfy their own ego. So, let's be attentive to the future events, and let us keep in our minds that this alleged alien attack will be a false flag attack.

II.5. The military-industrial complex.

This part of the book is dedicated to the skeptics, to all those who think that this ghost government, this invisible structure does not exist.

The first to mention the term **"military-industrial complex"** is the President Eisenhower. In his closing term speech, the 34th President of the United States, warns us about this invisible structure.

Here is an excerpt from his speech delivered on 17 January 1961 and broadcast via American television, the speech will enter to the literature under the name "Military-Industrial Complex Speech".

Excerpt:

"In the councils of government, we must guard against the acquisition of unwarranted influence, whether sought or unsought, by **the Military-Industrial Complex**. The potential for the disastrous rise of misplaced power exists and will persist."

His successor President Kennedy continues the fight against this occult structure. He will be unfortunately the last one. Here is an excerpt from his speech delivered on April 26, 1961 in New York City:

"The very word "secrecy" is repugnant in a free and open society; and we are as a people inherently and historically **opposed to secret societies,** to secret oaths and to secret proceedings...Our way of life is under attack. Those who make themselves our enemy are advancing around the globe...no war ever posed a greater threat to our security. If you are awaiting a finding of "clear and present danger," then I can only say that the danger has never been more clear and its presence has never been more imminent...For **we are opposed around the world by a monolithic and ruthless conspiracy** that relies primarily on covert means

217

for expanding its sphere of influence—on infiltration instead of invasion, on subversion instead of elections, on intimidation instead of free choice, on guerrillas by night instead of armies by day. It is a system which has conscripted vast human and material resources into the building of a tightly knit, highly efficient machine that combines military, diplomatic, intelligence, economic, scientific and political operations. Its preparations are concealed, not published. Its mistakes are buried, not headlined. Its dissenters are silenced, not praised. No expenditure is questioned, no rumor is printed, no secret is revealed."

We all know how JFK died.
50 years to the day after her great-grandfather speech, January 17, 2011, Laura Eisenhower takes up the torch. She us written in a long statement:

"Since my great-grandfather mentioned it for the first time fifty years ago, the military-industrial complex has flourished under the official seal of state secrecy, and even if there is some disclosure on its nature, this would consist very probably in a diversion that would not reveal never fully why this culture of secret flourished, nor what was done in our back all these years. At any rate, this

218

disclosure is unavoidable and is spreading throughout our ranks, and if we can understand and integrate other valuable truths, we will protect it against any disclosure used to introduce false concepts that would push back into of the mystification limbo".

The term 'military-industrial complex tripartite" describes this structure perfectly. "Tripartite" means, the military (and the military industry), the politicians and the mass media.

It's a structure that operate on a global scale. For the skeptics who still have doubts, here is a scale example of France, which is a good illustration of the relations between mass media, politicians and military industry.

We are in France, during the period of President Sarkozy

Who owns the media in France?

Even if the multitude of media and marks gives the impression of having a diversity and plurality in the media, after analysis, we realize that this is not the case.

Arnaud Lagardère, close friend of Nicolas

Sarkozy, described as "my brother" by the latter,

Lagardère group owns:

Editions Hachette, Fayard, Grasset, Hatier, Hazan, The Mask, Marabout, Plural, Stock, The Pocket Book, Larousse, Armand Colin, Dalloz and Dunod; Relay and Virgin stores;
The press titles: Paris-Match, Elle magazine, the Sunday newspaper, La Provence, Nice-Matin; radio stations Europe1, Europe 2, RFM; them TV channels: Canal J, MCM, Mezzo, Tiji, Match TV, the weather channel, CanalSatellite, Planet, Future Planet, Thalassa Planet, Channel Jimmy, Season, CinéCinéma, AlloCinéInfo and EuroChannel; among others.
Aeronautical industry group, major customer of public markets. Turnover in 2008: 8.2 Billions of Euro's.

Martin Bouygues, close friend of Nicolas Sarkozy and godfather of one of his sons.

The Bouygues group, which is basically a group of building and public works, major client of public markets. Turnover in 2008, 32.7 billion euros has:

The TV channels: TF1, LCI, Odyssée,

Eurosport, History, UshuaïaTV, S Star, Cinétoile, Cinéstar, Télétoon, Infosport, Series Club, TF6, TV Breizh.
Film production companies: Téléma, Film By Film, TF1 Film Production.
Film distribution companies: TFM.
THE video publishing company: TF1 Vidéo
The magazines: Tfou Mag, Star Academy. The free daily written press: Métro.

The arms dealer **Serge Dassault**, close by Nicolas Sarkozy. **The Dassault group** which is also a major client of the French public market possesses:

The press titles: Le Figaro, L'Express, Le Figaro Magazine and « Valeurs actuelles ».

The Bertelsmann group owns:

The RTL and M6 group channels.

Vivendi Universal owns:

The Vivendi group and tv channels Canal+ and SFR.

In other words, in the hands of only 5 large financial groups, whose owners of some are extremely close to the President of the French

Republic, we have the 1st publisher of France, the 2nd bookseller, the 1st daily newspaper, the 1st channel of French television.

Is it a coincidence?

Can we expect that a weapons merchant owned television channel to criticize the war? Or tell us that the terrorist threat is exaggerated? That the terrorist threat is invented? Of course not, this channel has every interest in exaggerating the terrorist threat and to glorify the war.
Can we expect, from a chain of television belonging to a financial group or a bank, to criticize the current economic system? Of course not, this chain must serve the interests of his masters.
Can we expect from this tripartite system at the service of his masters that he gives real information about a smart extraterrestrial life? Of course not, an extraterrestrial intelligent civilization would risk disrupt the established order.
We have also observed for several decades that this tripartite military-industrial complex has infiltrated the education. Education is considered today as one market among others and the works on which the works on which the education program is based, regardless of the country, are

222

unfortunately from the same publishers belonging to groups at the service of this system. Our schools and universities no longer care to train thinkers, poets, writers or other trades likely to challenge the system in place to improve it. They were unfortunately, gradually transformed into breeding institutions that train servant of the system. They only form that the system needs "soldiers".

So, you and me who tries to think, who points the problem, who tries to emancipate themselves from this one-track thinking because we have noticed that it can only lead us to our ruin, will be called paranoid, conspiratorial or crazy. The infiltration of our school system is the greatest danger for humanity but fortunately education does not stop school learning. We have a big responsibility as parents towards our children, it is incumbent upon us to open their eyes; and maybe a day will come when there will be many of us, more than the soldiers of the system, so as not to destroy this one but to improve it, to revise it by in relation to our priorities.

"A hidden faction of the government of an incredible power is keeping the UFO information secret."

Dick D'amato.

Chapter III: Contact.

"Eisenhower encountered aliens three times".

Timothy Good.

III.1. Why still no official contact?

According to the latest estimates, there would be
10 billion of planets similar to ours,
able to harbor an intelligent civilization,
only in our galaxy, the Milky way.
The age of our galaxy is estimated at 12 billion
years, that of our planet at 4.5 billion years.
we must also take into account that most of the
Milky way planets are at least 2 billion years older
than our planet, the galaxy should therefore
abound with intelligent civilizations.
So why this great silence. We are faced with a
paradox.
Paradox, also pointed out by Enrico Fermi, the
Italian physicist has not published work on the
subject but would have made a quick calculation
during a dialogue with one of his colleagues, and
according to him an intelligent civilization who

would be 1 to 2 billion years older than the ours
would have taken only 100 million years to
colonize our galaxy, however, it is not at all the
case. We will try to understand why, in 6 points.
In based on the conference of the Canadian
author Marc Séguin "The Fermi Paradox; where
are the extraterrestrial civilizations?" And on
multiple evidence that certify that there has
already been contact with these civilizations.
Let's take Albert Einstein's quote about God,
light and evil, Einstein said:

"Darkness is the absence of light"

so, if we find ourselves in a obscure place, we
cannot immediately deduce that light does not
exist, but only that the light is absent or missing.
About the extraterrestrials we are in lack of
official information. The trend is denial and
concealment.
From this voluntary official lack of information,
we cannot immediately deduce that the aliens do
not exist. But although information about them,
that we are entitled to know, is missing or absent.

1. The distance.

If we reduce the scale of the Universe to that of our Earth, and knowing that our sun is 100 times larger than the Earth. The sun would be reduced to the size of an orange, the nearest star Proxima Centauri, if you are within Paris would be in New York, and the second star there closer would be in an island in the Pacific Ocean. This distance would therefore block us, yes indeed, if we move with current earth technology this distance is impossible to navigate. It represents 4.25 light-years i.e. 40,000 billion km is 700,000 times the Earth-Mars distance. But an intelligent extraterrestrial civilization being 2 billion years ahead of us, and having followed the same pattern of evolution, should also master advanced transport technologies, like "using black holes" as interdimensional portals. For example, there are alien races that can create their own interdimensional portal. I had the chance to observe this phenomenon with my own eyes. These portals can get you to anywhere in a nanosecond, so distance is not a credible argument.

2. The prime directive.

A very advanced civilization will leave the chance to the less advanced civilizations to acquire a certain maturity before making contact with them. They would therefore observe our evolution without interfere and without assisting us with new technology. Like a balanced adult would in no case give a weapon to a child of 2 years. This civilization would be so wise and powerful, that it would prevent the colonization of these civilizations still in their infancy by more aggressive civilizations. Acting like cops of the Universe. This point joins the hypothesis, that the hidden face of the moon is colonized by a very advance species in relation to us and observes us. We are for the moment a civilization in quarantine.

This gives us a hint and seems to approve the President Eisenhower's contact with the first race of humanoids having him offered assistance to enable the human breed to reach a high psychic degree.

3. Conspiracy theory.

World leaders are complicit in a big conspiracy to hide the contact extraterrestrial. According to Canadian author Marc Séguin, our leaders are not even enough smart to hide their mistresses from the big public, so how could they hide such a huge secret. Marc Seguin has reason except that we are not talking about the same leaders.

Take, for example, the presidents of the United States. President Eisenhower and in a least extent President Kennedy have had the courage to challenge these shadow leaders.

Unfortunately, their successors will not have the same character traits. Without a doubt because the shadow government has since greatly consolidated his power. The leaders in question, whom they suspected to plot against humanity, are at the head of the global military-industrial-complex. Those leaders do not pledge allegiance to any country and operate in the shadows, and in no way a person elected for a 4-year term will have access to top secret information that may harm this cartel. The President of the United States and all the other world leaders are just mere temporary employees in their eyes, to expect some action from them, who being able to break this silence, would be a real miracle.

4. The planetarium hypothesis.

A civilization having of billions of years ahead of ours, would have built a dome giant around the Earth, simulating the planets and the stars. This giant dome would prevent us to observe that in reality the galaxy is full of intelligent civilization, and when the time comes, a times humans become more mature, these extraterrestrials would make contact.

This hypothesis seems the least likely to me.

5. The universal decline.

According to this hypothesis, civilizations having very advanced technology, after reaching some degree of knowledge, they self-destruct. We can quote here a nuclear war or other catastrophe related to technology and this cycle repeat itself eternally in the whole universe, so we're the only technologically advanced civilization in the universe.

This hypothesis seems to me rather improbable and particularly pessimistic.

6. an atypical development.

According to this hypothesis, what happened on Earth is a sequence of chance and the evolution on other planets even showing tremendous similarities to Earth, wouldn't have been as lucky at some point another of its evolution the chain of chance would be broken and life would be remained at a primary stage, microbial or animal. In any case not conducive to continuing to evolve into a technological civilization.
This hypothesis seems more down to earth, but very egocentric. They try to prove that the Human like the Earth is unique and that our universe which is a masterpiece of harmony mathematical, would be due to simple chance. So, there was a lot of luck. And I find it very hypocrite that people claim to be very smart, and wanting convincing proof and exceptional for aliens, suddenly starts to believe in coincidence.

III.2. The Blue City (allegory)

Shrink our galaxy to the size of our Earth, and imagine that this (our galaxy) is our Earth. What do you observe inside of it, all kinds of materials and objects. The world as you've always known, with these mountains, oceans, forests, deserts, rivers, seas... Apart from these natural formations, there are also a multitude of residential neighborhoods very diversified, cities, houses, villas, row houses, farms, some are inhabited others abandoned, dilapidated. Some are beautiful others not; and in a peaceful suburb at the Eastern end, far from the bustle and bustle of the center, a magnificent blue city (our planet).

Seen from afar, the blue city is a real gem. It's a pleasant place to live, these local residents, we humans, are highly diversified beings, such as its flora and its wildlife.

It has already been thousands of years that other inhabitants of Earth (our galaxy), have noticed the blue city and they have been watching it since a long time. They also visited, several times, to the ancestors of the inhabitants of the blue city, helping them with their knowledge and their technologies.

But in recent time, the inhabitants of the blue city have adopted a weird behavior. They no longer respected their City, observers can easily see that the city is increasingly polluted. So, they decide to infiltrate to take a closer look it. After some time, they find that the calm of the blue city is only a decoy, and that this blue jewel is a very violent place. The inhabitants are divided politically, religiously, economically, but also because of their skin colors and other physical attractions. They have a strange way to resolve their problems amongst themselves. They seem to prefer violence and war on dialogue and peace. The observers also note other anomalies. The city has all kinds of raw materials and other natural assets that can allow to have free energy and inexhaustible. But still strangely, the inhabitants do not exploit it, they prefer fossil energy, polluting and generating conflicts; it is as if the local residents had running water in their habitats but still preferred to go to the well for drinking water and to the river or lake meet other health needs. Yet the inhabitants of the city work hard and almost every day, and every time aera of peace sets in and the city can finally progress technologically, the inhabitants kill each other, strangely a conflict breaks out and the city regress, but they are brave and continue at work. After several years of observation, the undercover observers finally manage to detect the deception.

The inhabitants of the blue city are controlled by very ingenious systems and processes, by only 2% of its population.

These knowledge keepers control the access to the city. Getting out is impossible, anyway given the dilapidated habitats and the vast inhospitable regions surrounding it, what's the point of getting out of it; Moreover, the majority of residents are convinced that they are alone on Earth. The majority believe it but not all, residents more curious and with a critical mind tries to pierce the veil and get out of this one-track thinking.

They equip themselves with more and more instruments sophisticated, observe and report anomalies to their pair. But the knowledge keepers ridicule, calling them dreamy or even crazy. They are discredited and anyway their pseudoscience has no foundation.

One day during a conflict that will last for years,
the inhabitants of the city will explode two
bombs of such intensity that they will
do great damage, not only in the city but also to
the dwellings surrounding it.
The intensity of the bomb is so strong that it is
observed and heard by neighboring peoples
of the city, although they are very far away.
After that day, the peoples of the Earth observe
with particular attention the residents of this city
that unconscious of their acts will continue to
play with their new toy. Bombs will explode
regular intervals in the city. They will create
material damage but also large area of radiation.
External observers finding this a irresponsible
and inadmissible attitude, decide to contact the
leaders from the city.

The first people will appear and
will demand that these barbaric activities be
stopped and completely disarm the city; in
return, they will offer technological assistance
and accompaniment to allow this people, capable
of both the worst and the best, of acquiring the
wisdom and the technology needed to finally be
part of the big global family. The leaders too
preoccupied with intestines struggles will refuse

this offer. Our visitors will leave empty-handed but will continue to observe us while warning us against a second People apparently reputed to be dangerous. They will claim that pass one agreement with them will be to the detriment of inhabitants of the blue city. The second People physically very different from humans will arrive soon after and as predicted by the first, they will offer help technology without asking for the disarmament. They will come up with new types transport powered by energy free and a technology to control mentally the residents of the city, in counterpart the leaders of the city will have to provide humans, humans in large quantity for the experiments of this breed sick and wanting to find an antidote through of these experiences. The city leaders will see a boon of new technology against what the city possesses in abundance "of the human".

After that day the disappearances and testimonies kidnappings by this new breed will abound without finding official interlocutor in the city. Some better-informed residents will unite and will demand more transparency. And when the protest will grow, the guardians of the knowledge will fight the citizens with the police first then the army. But this time the inhabitants of the city are obstinate, they persevere in their struggle; for the knowledge keepers, these protestors are like barking dogs.

Their schedule is in no way affected.

Besides, the ruling class finds that the city is overcrowded and new technologies acquired, supposed at the base to free the residents of their labors produce daily new unemployed. The system must imperative to let go of ballast and get rid of these people who have become useless; and to do so, the cycle of terror aimed at maintaining the population in a state of permanently drowsiness and to reduce it resumes.

Knowledge keepers will provide local residents with the blue city a pandemic. The happy survivors will find themselves in the midst of crisis and economic recession. The cycle of terror will continue with terrorism, attacks under false banner will be perpetrated throughout the city. This Climate of hatred will lead to a great war. During and after the war, the conditions of hygiene that has become deplorable, will legitimize the advent of new viruses, and a new pandemic will emerge. The city will be again in economic crisis and this infernal cycle with sometimes a short moment of respite will follow until the ruling class reaches the expected results. And in the meantime, neighboring peoples continue to observe us, but without interfering in our internal problem, leaving us sometimes some signs of their presence.

If history would have followed its normal course, the inhabitants of the blue city should have been since a very long time in constant contact with a multitude of foreign peoples, but like a garden hose that would have been deliberately clogged, water (the normal course of history) is blocked and the pipe swells. One day it will explode or be outlet. It just depends on us.

III.3. Our World after a direct contact.

Let's imagine together that despite all the efforts of the tripartite military-industrial complex, that a extraterrestrial civilization unilaterally decides to make contact with the inhabitants of the Earth and forces the shadow rulers to disclose the truth. There is no doubt that the world in would be transformed.

1. The military-industrial complex, and its control mechanisms, that hold voluntarily Humanity in a state of drowsiness will disappear.

2. Humans would finally realize their cosmic nature and priorities will change.

3. Nuclear weapon and other components that could annihilate Humanity will be put Out of state of causing trouble.

4. Our understanding of the universe, of our genesis and our destiny will change.

5. We might have answers about the creation of man and on God.

6. Our values, our taboos, our motivations will change.

241

7. Our culture will be impacted and we will mutually enrich.

8. We could be part, as earthlings, of a new political alliance galactic trade.

9. New projects, new sciences and knowledge will render the old obsolete.

10. New technologies will make it possible to move into the cosmic era. From a local civilization and closed, we will turn into a cosmic explorer civilization.

11.This extraterrestrial contact will bring us together, we will all be representatives of the race human, that will put an end to all the xenophobic theories aimed at dividing us.

12. Thanks to new technologies, we could produce green and free energy.

13. Thanks to new agricultural technologies, we could end the famine.

14. Thanks to new green technologies we could eradicate pollution and restore the ecosystem of our planet.

15. New medical technologies
will allow Humanity to emancipate itself from
medical-pharmaceutical cartel.

The technology of extraterrestrial civilizations,
thousands or even billions of years old ahead of
us, is not limited to that, but first expect more
from them would be utopian. They will tell us
their technologies as we develop evolution.
Again, this will depend on us.

III.4. Conclusion.

We have just traveled together a multitude of information, all likely to approve that extraterrestrial life exists.

We found that statistically it is impossible that we are alone in this vast universe.

We have seen the traces of these extraterrestrial civilizations in cave paintings, in the holy writings, in art, in stories and cosmogonies of ancient tribes, in the relics of ancient civilizations, in testimonies, sightings and incidents of flying objects of non-terrestrial origin.

We also found based on stories of abductions and persons contacted that we are dealing with a multitude of races operating from very different way.

We analyzed the different theories, hypotheses and reflections dealing with the subject, to come to the statements of the ancient astronauts, soldiers and statesmen who are very valuable. We tried to bring answers to questions:

"Are we alone in the universe? »,
"What would happen to the human society after a contact directly with extraterrestrial civilizations? ", and
"Why still no official contact?".

If we can compare this situation to an information war, ufology would be an army weak and scattered in the face of the army of a great military power. The ufology needs a Saladin or of a Joan of Arc to be able to unite, win battles and finally disclose the truth to the World.

Sources.

1. www.messagesdelanature.ek.la/les-objets-fossiles-impossibles.
2. Freedom-news network
3. Documentaire SyFy les aliens sur la lune.
4. www.rtl.fr la vague belge d'ovnis
5.www.rtbf.be la vague belge d'ovnis
6.www.bfmtv.com
7. Documentaire « La conspiration d'Orion »
8. Documentaire « Unaknowledged »
9. Documentaire << Bob Lazard >>
10. Le matin des magiciens Jaques Bergiers et L.Pauwels.
11. Émission Tv sur TSR 1970, Jaques Bergiers
12 Documentaire «media de masse désinformation et manipulation du peuple »
13. www.gentinside.com 68
14. www.lesoleil.com
15. Galaktik diplomasi, Erhan Kolbasi.
16. siriusufo.org
17. Haktan Akdogan Youtube channel
18. Nasa.org.
19. www.defense.gov
20. www.spiegel.de
21. www.rr0.org
22. www.ovni-info-france.fr « la rumeur de

Roswell » de Pierre Lagrange

23. Laura Eisenhower YouTube channel

24. Chariots of Gods. Erich Von Däniken

25. L'empreinte des dieux. Graham Hancock.

26. www.science.howstuffworks.com

27. www.dailynebraskan.com

28. www.onlyinyourstate.com

29 .Article paru dans le journal Nebraska Nugget.
The cowboys heard a « Terrific whirring noise. »

30 .www.edn.com «< ghost-rocket >>

31. www.thelocal.se « host rocket >>

32 .www.deccanchronicle.com ghost rockets over Scandinavia

33. Ufos and government: a historical inquiry. Michael D.Swords.

34.The ufo dossier: 100 years of government secrets, conspiracies, and cover-UPS. Kevin D.Randle.

35 .www.scienceetavenir.fr que s est il passé à Toungouska en 1908.

36. www.phys.org researchers say Tunguska event was an ufo crash.

37. www.courierinternational.com Toungouska un ovni scientifique vieux de 100 ans.

38. www.mercuredegaillon.free.fr liste de plus de
100 craches UFOR du CSETI.

39 www.ufologiemaranormal.org Gdynia ufo crash.

40. Perceptions Magazine. Mai 2000. Interview de Robert O.Dean par Randy Koppang.

41. www.icietmaintenant.fr récupération d epave
en Allemagne 1974.

42. Livre secret russe sur les races extraterrestres.
Introduction to the alien races book.

43. www.mowxml.org livre secret russe des races
extraterrestres

44. www.exopolitics.blogs.com introduction the alien races book.

45. www.astrosurf.com le défi des ovnis

46. Les O.V.N.I. Michel Dorier, Jean Pierre Troadec.

47. Presence ovni, crop circles et exocivilisations
de Denis Roger Denocla.

48. The Aliens and the Scalpel de Roger K.Leir.

49. www.home.tothestarsacademy.com

50. www-lexpress-fr.cdn.ampproject.org
www.lexpress.fr culture théories folles de 1 histoire l'énigme de la grande pyramide.

51. Interview Laura Eisenhower and R. Wayne

Steiger youtube.

52. R Wayne Steiger YouTube channel.
53. www.sciencepost.fr
54. www.maxisciences.com peintures rupestres
55. www.icomos.org. « Peintures rupestres
Chhatisgarh >>.
56. www.ahriman.fr << ovni et alien dans l art
»
57. www.jeanluclamaire.fr ovni dans les
Ardennes peintures rupestres.
58. www.futurascience.com << les peintures
rupestres l art des chasseurs collecteurs »
59. www.astrosurf.com «l'astronomie des
dogons »
60. www.sceptique.qc.ca « Sirius et les dogons
».
61. www.un.org databases
62. www.cia.gov ufos photos
63. www.fbi.gov the vault ufo FBI records
64. Documentaire « médias et réalité petit
guide de manipulation de masse out the box »
youtube.

65. Les livres Saint : Le Saint Coran, la Bible «
ancien testament », le Mahabharata, le Dyzan
tibétain, l'avesta, le Srimad Bhagasvatam, le
Ramayana, le sanskritSamaranagana
Sutradhara.

Printed in Great Britain
by Amazon

19724354R00144